The Specials, also known as The Special AKA, are an English 2 tone & ska reviv[al band formed in] 1977 in Coventry, England, UK. Following some early changes, their 1st stable [line-up was Terry Hall &] Neville Staple on vocals, Lynval Golding & Roddy Radiation on guitars, Horace Panter on bass, Jerry Dammers on keyboards, John Bradbury on drums, and Dick Cuthell & Rico Rodriguez on horn. Their music combines a "danceable ska and rocksteady beat with punk's energy & attitude". Lyrically, they have a "focused and informed political & social stance".

The Specials' members wore mod-style "'60s rude boy outfits of pork pie hats, tonic and mohair suits & loafers". Too Much Too Young, the lead track on their The Special AKA Live! EP, topped the UK Singles Chart in 1980, as did Ghost Town, about the recession in Britain the following year. After 7 UK top 10 singles in a row from 1979 - 1981, main lead vocalists Terry and Neville, along with guitarist Lynval, left to form Fun Boy Three.

Continuing as The Special AKA, a name that they'd often used on earlier Specials records, a much changed line-up released new material until 1984, including the top 10 UK single Free Nelson Mandela. Founder & songwriter Dammers then folded the band, becoming a political activist. The Specials re-formed during 1993, having continued to perform and record with varying line-ups, none of them involving Jerry.

The group was formed in 1977 by songwriter/keyboardist Dammers, vocalist Tim Strickland, guitarist/vocalist Lynval Golding, drummer Silverton Hutchinson & bassist Horace Panter, a.k.a. Sir Horace Gentleman. Tim was replaced by Terry Hall shortly after the band's formation, first being named the Automatics then the Coventry Automatics. Vocalist Neville Staple and guitarist Roddy Byers, known as Roddy Radiation, joined the group the following year, the new line-up changing their name to the Special AKA. Joe Strummer, who'd seen one of their gigs, invited them to open for the Clash on their On Parole UK tour, which increased their national exposure, the 2 bands briefly sharing the same management.

The Specials began at the same time as Rock Against Racism, which was 1st organised during 1978. Jerry stated that anti-racism was intrinsic to their formation, the group having the goal of integrating black & white folk. Many years later he said that "Music gets political when there are new ideas in music, ...punk was innovative, so was ska, and that was why bands such as the Specials & the Clash could be political".

Shortly after drummer Silverton Hutchinson left the group to be replaced by John Bradbury, Dammers formed the 2 Tone Records label, issuing their first single Gangsters, which made the UK Top 10 that summer, being a reworking of Prince Buster's 'Al Capone'. They'd begun wearing mod/rude boy/skinhead-style 2-tone tonic suits, along with other elements of late '60s teen fashions. Changing their name to the Specials, they recorded their eponymous debut L.P. in 1979, produced by Elvis Costello. Horn players Dick Cuthell and Rico Rodriguez were featured on the disc, but didn't join the Specials until their 2nd album.

The Specials led off with Dandy Livingstone's 'Rudy, A Message to You', having slightly altered the title to 'A Message to You, Rudy, also covering Prince Buster and Toots & the Maytals songs from the late '60s. The EP Too Much Too Young, credited to the Special A.K.A. was UK Singles Chart topper during 1980, its lyrics being controversial, referring to teenage pregnancy, promoting contraception.

Going back to the Specials name, the band's 2nd L.P., More Specials, didn't sell as well, being recorded at a time when Terry said that conflicts had developed in the group. Female backing vocalists on the Specials' first 2 studio albums included Chrissie Hynde; Rhoda Dakar of the Bodysnatchers then the Special AKA; and Belinda Carlisle, Jane Wiedlin & Charlotte Caffey of the Go-Go's. The band had a break from recording and touring for the 1st few months of 1981 then released Ghost Town, which hit No. 1 that year.

At their Top of the Pops recording of the song, Staple, Hall and Golding announced that they were leaving the group. Lynval later said: "We didn't talk to the rest of the guys. We couldn't even stay in the same dressing room. We couldn't even look at each other. We stopped communicating. You only realise what a genius Jerry was years later. At the time, we were on a different planet". Shortly afterwards the trio left the Specials to form Fun Boy Three.

The band was in a state of flux over the next few years. Adding Rhoda Dakar to their permanent line-up, they recorded The Boiler with her on vocals, Dammers on keyboards, Bradbury on drums, John Shipley from the Swinging Cats on guitar, Dick Cuthell on brass & Nicky Summers on bass. The single, credited to Rhoda with the Special AKA, featured a frank, harrowing description of a date rape, severely limiting its airplay, but it made UK No. 35. American writer Dave Marsh rated The Boiler as one of the 1,001 best 'rock 'n' soul' singles of all time in his book The Heart of Rock & Soul.

After going on tour with Rodriguez, the group, sans Dakar, as 'Rico and the Special AKA' also recorded the non-charting, non-album single Jungle Music. The line-up for the single was Rodriguez (vocal, trombone), Dick (cornets), Jerry (keyboards), John Bradbury (drums), John Shipley (guitar) & returning bassist Horace Panter, along with new additions Satch Dickson and Groco (percussion) & Anthony Wymshurst (guitar).

Rico and the 3 newcomers were all dropped for the next single, War Crimes, which brought back Rhoda & added new vocalists Egidio Newton and Stan Campbell, plus violinist Nick Parker. Follow-up single Racist Friend made UK No. 60, with the band establishing themselves as a septet: Dakar, Newton, Campbell, Bradbury, Cuthell, Dammers & Shipley. The new line-up, still known as the Special AKA, issued a new full-length L.P. In the Studio in 1984.

The group was officially now a sextet: Dakar, Campbell, Bradbury, Dammers, Shipley and new bassist Gary McManus. Cuthell, Newton, Panter & Roddy Radiation all featured on the album as guests; as did saxophonist Nigel Reeve, along with Claudia Fontaine and Caron Wheeler of the vocal trio Afrodiziak. In The Studio wasn't as successful as their previous L.Ps, both critically & commercially, but the single Free Nelson Mandela hit UK No. 9 during 1984, helping to make Mandela's imprisonment a cause célèbre in Britain, also becoming popular with anti-apartheid activists in South Africa. Jerry then dissolved the band to pursue political activism, before forming a large, jazz-style ensemble, the Spatial AKA Orchestra, in 2006.

Many members of the The Specials have played in other groups since the break-up, having reformed several times to tour and record in Specials-related projects, but there's never been a complete reunion of the original line-up. Following their departure from the Specials, Golding, Hall & Staple founded the pop band Fun Boy Three, being successful from 1981 - 1983 with hits including Tunnel of Love, It Ain't What You Do (It's the Way That You Do It), Our Lips Are Sealed and The Lunatics (Have Taken Over the Asylum). The group ended with Terry's sudden departure, leading to a 15-yr rift with Neville.

After Fun Boy Three, Staple & Lynval joined Pauline Black of the Selecter in the short-lived band Sunday Best, releasing the single Pirates on the Airwaves. Bradbury, Golding, Panter and Neville teamed up with members of the Beat in 1990 to form Special Beat, performing music from the 2 groups along with other ska & Two Tone classics. They toured and issued several live recordings during the '90s, going through many line-up changes.

A single credited to 'X Specials' featuring Staple, Golding, Radiation, and Panter came out in '94. Their cover of Slade's hit Coz I Love You, was produced by Slade's Jim Lea. Moving into production & management, Neville 'discovered' and produced bhangra pop fusion artist Johnny Zee. Staple produced & guested with many artists during the '80s and '90s, including International Beat, Special Beat, Unwritten Law, Desorden Publico & the Planet Smashers, as well as leading his own bands and starting the Rude Wear clothing line. He sang with the '90s Specials line-up then again from 2009 to 2012.

Horace went on to join up with members of the Beat & Dexys Midnight Runners to form General Public then Special Beat. He joined the '90s Specials before training as a primary school teacher at the University of Central England in Birmingham. Panter played bass with latter-day Special Neol Davies in the blues group Box of Blues then rejoined the Specials for their 2009 reunion, continuing to be a member.

Lynval teamed up with Jerry for a brief spell of club DJing, before playing guitar with Coventry band After Tonight. After Special Beat, he went on to lead the Seattle-based ska groups Stiff Upper Lip they Pama International, as well as collaborating with many other ska bands, having also toured with the Beat. Golding joined the '90s Specials line-up, leaving in the year 2000 then rejoining during 2009, continuing to play guitar with the group.

Roddy fronted and played guitar with many artists including the Tearjerkers, a band that he'd started in the last months of the Specials, the Bonediggers, the Raiders and Three Men & Black, including Jean-Jacques Burnel of the Stranglers, Jake Burns (Stiff Little Fingers), Pauline Black, Bruce Foxton (the Jam), Dave Wakeling (the Beat, General Public) and Nick Welsh (Skaville UK). Radiation also fronts the Skabilly

Rebels, a group that mixes rockabilly with ska. He joined the '90s Specials line-up then again in 2009, continuing to play guitar until 2014.

Bradbury drummed through the Special AKA era then formed the band JB's Allstars, before moving into production. He joined Special Beat for several years then a reformed Selecter, before retiring from music to work as an IT specialist. John rejoined the Specials for their 2009 reunion, continuing to perform with them until his death during 2015.

Terry fronted the Colourfield from 1984 - 1987, who had some success, pursuing a solo career after they broke up, working mostly in the new wave genre. He co-wrote a number of early Lightning Seeds releases, also singing some vocals on a Dub Pistols album. Hall & Eurythmics member David A. Stewart formed the duo Vegas in the early '90s, putting out an eponymous L.P. during '92. He joined the Specials for their 2009 reunion, continuing to sing with them.

The 1st reunion of The Specials took place in 1993, when producer Roger Lomas was asked by Trojan Records to get some musicians together to back ska legend Desmond Dekker on a new album. He approached all their members, the only 4 wanting to take part being Roddy Radiation, Neville Staple, Lynval Golding and Horace Panter, who were joined by Aitch Bembridge, who'd drummed for The Selecter. Aitch had played with soul singer Ray King during the '70s, who mentored & worked with Jerry, Neville, Lynval & drummer Silverton in their days before the Specials. A group of studio musicians filled out the band, including keyboardist Mark Adams. The album, issued by Trojan Records as King of Kings, was credited to Desmond Dekker and the Specials.

The release of the L.P. with Desmond Dekker created a buzz for the group, leading to a Japanese promoter's offer to book a tour. Rejoined by Golding, along with Aitch Bembridge & Adams from the King of Kings sessions, the band added horn players Adam Birch and Jonathan Read then began rehearsing & playing live. After calling themselves the Coventry Specials, The X Specials and Specials2, they soon reverted to The Specials, as the promoters were using the name anyway, although the line-up was referred to as Specials MkII by those involved.

They went on tour internationally & put out a couple of studio L.Ps: Today's Specials, a collection of mainly reggae and ska covers in '96 then Guilty 'til Proved Innocent! during '98, an album of original compositions. The group toured intensively to support both records, including headlining the Vans Warped Tour, getting positive reviews of their live shows. Despite the live success, the band fizzled out after a tour of Japan in 1998 that Panter missed due to illness, although limited touring with a different line-up continued into the year 2000. The release of the earlier Trojan sessions, Skinhead Girl during 2000 then Conquering Ruler the following year would be their last for some time.

Having finished a similar project with The Selecter in 1999, Roger Lomas took the band back into the studio to record classic songs from the Trojan Records back catalogue. Lynval left the band a fortnight before this project, to spend more time with his family in Seattle. They replaced him on guitar with another Selecter veteran, Neol Davies, who together with Staple, Roddy & Horace, was joined by session musicians to record many tracks that were put out by Trojan sub-label Receiver Records as Skinhead Girl during the year 2000 then Conquering Ruler in 2001.

Hall teamed up with Golding for the first time in 24 years during 2007, to play Specials songs at a couple of music festivals. At Glastonbury Festival they were on the Pyramid Stage with Lily Allen performing Gangsters. Lynval said in May 2009 that Lily reuniting him with Terry played a "massive part" in the group's later reformation. Later that same day they played on the Park Stage, with Damon Albarn of Blur on piano and beatboxer Shlomo providing rhythm, to perform A Message to You, Rudy. At GuilFest, Golding joined the Dub Pistols to again perform Gangsters. Lynval regularly performed concerts during 2007 & recorded with Pama International, a collective of musicians who were members of Special Beat.

Hall revealed on 30th March 2008 that the Specials would be reforming for tour dates that autumn, possibly also doing some recording, which was officially confirmed on 7th April. Six members of the band performed on the main stage at the Bestival on 6th September, billed as the 'Surprise Act'. The group had announced tour dates by December 2008 to celebrate their 30th anniversary the following year, although founder member Dammers wasn't joining them on tour.

Terry said, "The door remains open to him". However, Jerry described the new reunion as a "takeover", stating that he'd been forced out of the band. Longtime Specials fan Amy Winehouse joined Dammers onstage in Hyde Park, singing the song that he'd written for the Specials, Free Nelson Mandela, for his 90th birthday concert, dubbed 46664 after Mandela's prison number, which was also the name of his AIDS charity, which received money raised by the concert.

The Specials guested on BBC 2's Later... with Jools Holland on 10th April 2009. The following month Bradbury and Golding stated that they planned to issue further original Specials material. It was announced on 8th June that the Specials would be embarking on a 2nd leg of their 30th anniversary tour, taking in the places & venues that they'd missed earlier in the year. The group toured Australia and Japan that July - August then received the Inspiration Award at the Q Awards in October. They performed at the Dutch festival Lowlands during 2010.

Hall confirmed at the Green Room, Manchester in November that there'd be further Specials dates during the autumn of 2011, saying that he'd enjoyed playing live again: "It's a celebration of something that happened in your life that was important & we're going to do that again next year, but then maybe that'll be it". The band re-released A Message to You, Rudy in late 2010 as a Haiti Special Fund available to download from iTunes in the UK & US, with proceeds going to the UNICEF effort to help children in Haiti following a devastating earthquake.

It was announced during February 2012 that the Specials would perform at Hyde Park with Blur and New Order to celebrate that year's Summer Olympics closing ceremony in London. Panter said that the group were excited to be involved in such a momentous event: "We've been keeping it under our pork pie hats for a month or so now. I think it's going to be the only chance folk get to see the Specials performing in the UK this year". The band's performance was said to have been synonymous with Britain's political & social upheaval of the late '70s - early '80s.

The group issued More... Or Less. – The Specials Live in August 2012, featuring 'the best of the best' performances from their European tour of the previous year, which they selected themselves, on a double-disc CD and double-vinyl L.P. The band announced the departure of Staple with the following message on their website during January 2013: "We're very sad that Neville can't join us on the Specials' UK tour in May 2013 or indeed on the future projects that we've planned. He's made a huge contribution to the fantastic time and reception that we've received since we started & reformed during 2009. However, he missed a number of key shows last year due to ill health, and his health is obviously much more important. We wish him the very best for the future".

The Specials completed a North American tour in 2013, performing to sold-out crowds in Chicago, Los Angeles, San Diego, San Francisco, Seattle, Portland & Vancouver. It was revealed during February 2014 that Roddy Radiation had left the reformed group. They played an extensive tour that autumn with Steve Cradock of Ocean Colour Scene as lead guitarist.

Drummer John Bradbury died on 28th December 2015 at the age of 62. The Specials announced on 22nd March 2016 that The Libertines drummer Gary Powell would be performing on their upcoming tours but he was replaced by PJ Harvey/Jazz Jamaica drummer Kenrick Rowe on the Encore album then following tour. The band invited 20 yr old brummie Saffiyah Khan to a show in 2017, after a photo of her confronting an 'English Defence League goon' in a Specials t-shirt at a counter-demonstration went viral. Less than 2 years later, Khan had performed on stage for the 1st time, recorded a song and toured North America with the group.

The Specials announced a UK tour during 2019 to coincide with the issue of their latest L.P., Encore on 29th October 2018. The band announced a Spring North American tour on 1st February 2019 to promote the release of Encore that day on Island Records. The following week Encore debuted at the top of the UK chart, their first # 1 album since 1980. The group invited 17-yr-old artist & photographer Sterling Chandler to photograph them on the remaining leg of their tour late that year. The Specials announced a UK tour in March 2021. Horace Panter announced a new 12-track Specials L P. on 7th July that was issued on 23rd August, titled Protest Songs 1924–2012. Vocalist Hannah Hu joined the band for their 2021 tour, having also sung on their new album.

Members

Current members

Lynval Golding – rhythm guitar, vocals (1977–81, 1993, 1994–1998, 2008–present)

Horace Panter – bass guitar (1977–81, 1982, 1993, 1994–1998, 2000-2001, 2008–present)

Terry Hall – vocals (1977–81, 2008–present)

Current touring musicians

Tim Smart – trombone (2008–present)

Nikolaj Torp Larsen – keyboards (2008–present)

Steve Cradock – lead guitar (2014–present)

Pablo Mendelssohn – trumpet (2014–present)

Kenrick Rowe – drums (2019–present)

Hannah Hu – backing vocals (2021–present)

Stan Samuel – rhythm guitar (2021–present)

Sid Gauld – trumpet (2021–present)

Former members

The Coventry Automatics

Silverton Hutchinson – drums (1977–79)

Tim Strickland – vocals (1977)

The Specials (original line-up)

Jerry Dammers – keyboards, principal songwriter (1977–84)

Roddy Radiation – lead guitar, vocals (1978–81, 1993, 1996–2001, 2008–14)

Neville Staple – toasting, vocals, percussion (1978–81, 1993, 1996–2001, 2008–12)

John Bradbury – drums (1979–84, 2008–15; his death)

Dick Cuthell – flugel horn (1979–84)

Rico Rodriguez – trombone (1979–81, 1982; died 2015)

The Special A.K.A.

Rhoda Dakar – vocals (1981–82, 1982–84)

John Shipley – guitar (1981–84)

Satch Dixon – percussion (1982)

Tony 'Groco' Uter – percussion (1982)

Anthony Wimshurst – guitar (1982)

Stan Campbell – vocals (1982–84)

Egidio Newton – vocals, percussion (1982–83)

Nick Parker – violin (1982)

Gary McManus – bass guitar (1983–84)

The Specials Mk.2. (1993-1998)

Jon Read – trumpet, percussion, bass (1996–1998, 2008–14)

Adam Birch – trumpet (1996–1998)

Mark Adams – keyboards (1993, 1994–1998)

Kendell – vocals (1998)

Charley Harrington Bembridge (Aitch Hyatt) – drums (1993, 1994–1998)

Trojan era Specials

Neol Davies – rhythm guitar, vocals (2000-2001)

Anthony Harty - drums, percussion (2000-2001)

Justin Dodsworth - keyboards (2000-2001)

Steve Holdway - trombone (2000-2001)

Paul Daleman - trumpet (2000-2001)

Leigh Malin - tenor sax (2000-2001)

The Specials (2008-present)

Drew Stansall – saxophone, flute (2008–2012)

Gary Powell – drums (2016–2019)

Discography

As The Specials

The Specials (1979)

More Specials (1980)

Today's Specials (1996)

Guilty 'til Proved Innocent! (1998)

Skinhead Girl (2000)

Conquering Ruler (2001)

Encore (2019)

Protest Songs 1924-2012 (2021)

As The Special A.K.A.

In the Studio (1984)

Further reading

Williams, Paul (1995) You're Wondering Now – A History of the Specials, ST Publishing. ISBN 1-898927-25-1

Panter, Horace (2007) Ska'd for Life – A Personal Journey with the "Specials", Sidgwick & Jackson, ISBN 978-0-283-07029-7

Chambers, Pete (2008) 2-Tone-2: Dispatches from the Two Tone City, 30 Years on, Tencton Planet Publications. ISBN 978-0-9544125-6-2

Staple, Neville (2009) Original Rude Boy, Aurum Press. ISBN 978-1-84513-480-8

Williams, Paul (2009) You're Wondering Now-The Specials From Conception to Reunion, Cherry Red Books. ISBN 978-1-901447-51-4

Thompson, Dave (2011) Wheels Out of Gear: 2-Tone, the Specials and a World In Flame, Soundcheck Books. ISBN 978-0-9566420-2-8

It didn't often happen, but pop singles occasionally had a startling ability to sum up the mood of their times. The Beatles' All You Need Is Love encapsulated the blissed-out, dippy logic of the Summer of Love during '67. The Pet Shop Boys' Opportunities (Let's Make Lots of Money) offered an arch deconstruction of the yuppie dream 20 yrs later: a suitably cynical record for a cynical era.

However, no record had captured the spirit of its age quite as acutely as The Specials' Ghost Town, which remained the most remarkable British chart-topper. Despairing of rising unemployment & frustrated by the most unpopular government of the post-war era, it wasn't only a peculiarly unsettling record, but a uniquely prescient one. As Ghost Town hit # 1, its lyrics were horribly borne out. 'Can't go on no more', sang the Specials, 'the people getting angry', just as the worst mainland rioting of the 20th century broke out in British cities. For once, British pop music seemed to be commenting on the news as it happened.

"Everything else in the charts was starting to go a bit Human League. Ghost Town summed up how much exciting stuff was going on in the town during punk. Clearly the Specials and a whole generation had been hugely inspired by what had happened with punk, culturally, socially & politically, but what had it led to? Synthesizers and floppy haircuts", said Billy Bragg, the UK's leading political songwriter, who in the summer of 1981 had just left the army.

The Specials were formed as the Coventry Automatics in 1977, when Jerry Dammers, the keyboardist son of a clergyman, asked bassist Horace Panter, another student at Lanchester Polytechnic, to help him record his self-penned reggae songs. They recruited musicians from Coventry's thriving club circuit: Jamaican-born guitarist Lynval Golding, who'd played in local soul bands, singer Terry Hall & guitarist Roddy 'Radiation' Byers, faces on the punk scene. Jerry's flatmate John Bradbury was drafted in on drums then their roadie Neville Staples, a former member of disco-dancing troupe Neville and the Boys, plugged in a microphone during a gig then began chatting along with the music.

They released their self-financed 1st single, Gangsters, during early 1979. Just a year later they were one of the UK's most successful groups, with 5 top 10 singles, Too Much Too Young having topped the charts in January 1980 & a hit L.P. Their success had led to its own genre and youth cult, Two Tone: the name of the Specials' record label & a nod to their multi-racial line-up. The charts featured other bands including The Selecter, Madness, the Beat and Bad Manners who imitated their punky, politicised take on ska, the long-neglected precursor to reggae, which had been popular in Jamaica during the '60s.

The Specials 2nd album, More Specials, was a daring, audacious attempt to add jazz & easy listening muzak to the Two Tone stew, which hit # 5. "Punk was dying, the Sex Pistols had split, the charts were full of 2nd-division punk groups and folk were after something new. We were in the right place at the right time & we had the tunes", said Horace Panter, a special needs teacher.

The Specials embarked on their More Specials tour in autumn 1980, a band at the top of their game. It should've been a golden time, but as their bus ploughed around England, the Specials were self-destructing. Relations between the members were at a low: they'd endured a gruelling schedule for over a year, and the sessions for More Specials had been spectacularly stormy. The tour was marred by audience violence which disrupted gigs in Newcastle, Leeds and Cambridge. At Cambridge, Hall & Dammers tried to stop fans battling with security guards, the pair being arrested, charged with incitement to riot then fined £400. "What started out as a big party ended up like One Flew Over the Cuckoo's Nest", said Roddy Byers.

"Everyone was getting under pressure and the band was getting tired. It wasn't just that, the country was falling apart. You travelled from town to town & what was happening was terrible. In Liverpool, all the shops were shuttered up, everything was closing down. Margaret Thatcher had apparently gone mad, she was closing down all the industries, throwing millions of people on the dole. We could actually see it by touring around. You could see that frustration and anger in the audience. In Glasgow, there were these little old ladies on the streets selling all their household goods, their cups & saucers. It was unbelievable. It was clear that something was very, very wrong", stated Jerry.

The roots of Ghost Town went back further, to the Specials' 1st major UK tour. During 1978, when still a good time local reggae group, they'd got a foot-of-the bill support slot with the Clash. However, in Bracknell the gig was disrupted by neo-Nazi skinheads allied to rabble-rousing street punks Sham 69. Losing at the polling stations with the rise of Margaret Thatcher, the National Front had instigated a programme of 'direct action', infiltrating football hooligans and skinheads: 'bovver' at gigs and matches was the far right's new route into the headlines. Earlier that year, seig heiling skinheads had done £7,500 worth of damage at a Sham 69 concert at the London School of Economics.

"In Bracknell, the Sham Army turned up, got onstage then attacked the lead singer of Suicide, the other support band. That was the night the Specials concept was born. I idealistically thought, 'We have to get through to these people'. It was obvious that a mod & skinhead revival was coming, so I was trying to find a way to make sure that it didn't go the way of the National Front and the British Movement. I saw punk as a piss-take of rock music, as rock music comitting suicide & it was great, it was really funny, but I couldn't believe folk took it as a serious musical genre which they then had to copy. It seemed to be a bit more healthy to have an integrated kind of British music, rather than white people playing rock and black folk playing their music. Ska was an integration of the two", said Dammers.

A year after the Bracknell gig, the Specials' eponymous debut L.P. set out their stall, its cover featuring them in the mod uniform of tonic suits, loafers & pork pie hats. Inside, simplistic pleas for racial tolerance were set to the choppy beat of ska, popular with the skinhead cult in the '60s. The album dealt in social realism. Despite their complaints that London was burning with boredom, most punk bands had kept a whiff of metropolitan glamour.

However, Terry Hall's vocals described a grimly provincial world of shopping precincts and shabby ballrooms in a deadpan Coventry whine. The L.P. also showed the group's ability to define the preoccupations of post-punk youth - the NF are on the march, teddy boys & punks punch it out, 'boot boys' lurk in the shadows, waiting to strike. It was a talent that came to its fullest fruition on Ghost Town, as would Jerry's plan to create "a weird new music that was a Jamaican-British crossover".

He'd begun experimenting with their trademark ska sound on their 2nd L.P., More Specials. Not all the members were enthused by Dammers' attempts to fuse reggae with easy listening. "He wanted to do this sort of muzak thing, put drum machines on everything. He'd been right up to that point, but I started to think that he was losing it a bit", said Roddy Byers. Rows erupted in the studio. "It was horrible. Every day somebody left the band", added Lynval Golding.

The acrimony spilled over into live performances, Roddy smashing his guitar over Jerry's keyboard during one show. There were further pressures on the group, Lynval being seriously injured in a racist attack in south London, an incident that inspired Ghost Town's B-side, Why? Dammers wouldn't discuss their drug use in depth, but said that there was "too much drink in the dressing room, too many drugs".

He also thought that the Specials' penchant for inviting their audience to invade the stage during concerts had got out of hand: "At first it started off, it was a great laugh: we're all in this together, there's no stars here. Then gradually, folk were getting onstage 2 numbers into the set and it became tedious and dangerous. In the end, the whole audience wanted to be onstage, the PA stacks were swaying & it was dangerous, but you couldn't stop it. We told the audience that it was too dangerous but they wouldn't have it then it ended up in a massive ruck with the bouncers".

Following the Cambridge debacle, the Specials announced that they'd stop touring. "You're in this amazing, fantastic band making this wonderful music but you can't play it any more because people are hitting each other", said Panter. Disillusioned with life as a Special, he joined a religious cult, Exegesis, which preached self-assertion, creating even more friction in the group. "Just to add to the fun and games, Horace joins some nutty cult & starts giving them all his money. It was a nightmare", recalled Jerry.

By the time the Specials met during early 1981 to record Ghost Town, the band was in its death throes. "Everybody was stood in different parts of this huge room with their equipment, no one talking. Jerry stormed out a couple of times virtually in tears and I went after him, 'Calm down, calm down'. It was hell to be around", remembered Horace.

Inspired by the scenes that Dammers had glimpsed in Glasgow, Ghost Town was powered by despair & anger at the state of the nation: 'Government leaving the youth on the shelf, no job to be found in this country', intoned Neville Staples, his voice gloomy, thick with West Indian patois. It was also the Specials' decision to quit touring: 'bands won't play no more, too much fighting on the dancefloor'.

The single's stark lyrical vision was set against an unique musical backdrop. Ghost Town had a loping reggae beat topped with eerie, jazz chords, stabbing horns influenced by soundtrack composer John Barry and instead of a chorus, a harrowing wail, which Dammers said was "supposed to sound a bit middle eastern, like a prophecy of doom". Once again, the sessions were fraught, as Jerry recalled:

"People weren't cooperating. Ghost Town wasn't a free-for-all jam session. Every little bit was worked out, composed, all the different parts. I'd been working on it for at least a year, trying out every conceivable chord. It was a combination of the 1st album & the 2nd L.P., the complete history of the group gelled in one song. I can remember walking out of a rehearsal in total despair because Neville wouldn't try the ideas.

The brass bit is kind of jazzy, it has a dischord. I remember Lynval rushing into the control room while they were doing it going, 'No, no, no, it sounds wrong! Wrong! Wrong!' In the meantime, Roddy's trying to kick a hole through the wall from the control room to the studio room. It was only a little studio in Leamington and the engineer was going, 'If that doesn't stop, you're going to have to leave!' I was saying, 'No! No! This is the greatest record that's ever been made in the history of anything! You can't stop now!'"

'Can't go on no more, the people getting angry': those lines could've referred to the the situation in the Leamington studio but as the Specials argued, events in the country were developing at a dramatic rate. Unemployment had risen from 1.5m to 2.5m in a year, among ethnic minorities it had gone up by 82%. In the first week of April '81 police in Brixton had introduced a stop & search policy, named Operation Swamp after Margaret Thatcher's assertion in '78 that Britain "might be rather swamped by people of a different culture". In six days, 943 people - the vast majority of them black - were stopped by plainclothes officers. The 1st rioting in Brixton broke out on April 10th. Ten days later over 100 people were arrested and 15 police injured in confrontations in Finsbury Park, Forest Gate & Ealing.

There were also 350 arrests in incidents outside the capital. An Asian teenager, Samtam Gill, was murdered in a racist attack in Coventry then in fighting between skinheads and ethnic minorities, police made 80 arrests. The Specials announced that they'd play a concert in Coventry for racial unity on the day that Ghost Town came out, June 20th. The National Front announced a march through the city on the same day. "The gig was half-full. There were rumours the NF was going to turn up & attack", said Panter.

Britain erupted on July 10th, as a 2nd wave of rioting in Brixton spread through the country, Southall, Battersea, Dalston, Streatham and Walthamstow in London, Handsworth in Birmingham, Chapeltown in

Leeds, Highfields in Leicester, Ellesmere Port, Luton, Sheffield, Portsmouth, Preston, Newcastle, Derby, Southampton, Cirencester, Nottingham, High Wycombe, Bedford, Edinburgh, Wolverhampton, Stockport, Blackburn, Bolton, Huddersfield, Halifax, Reading, Chester, Cardiff and Aldershot all reporting 'riots'.

The next day, Ghost Town hit # 1, developing a terrible currency that even Dammers couldn't have predicted. "It was an incredible moment. I can remember Rico saying, 'Jerry, if your army combine with my army, it's a revolution!'" "It floated on a tide of what was going on in society. If you think of songs that are expressly political, like Robert Wyatt's Shipbuilding, did its political content keep it from getting to the top of the charts & did Ghost Town sneak up there because it wasn't overtly political? What's being expressed in that song? Nothing's happening, everything's going down the pan, it's that classic no future, nihilistic punk thing. Ghost Town might well have been the only punk number one," stated Billy Bragg.

However, its success couldn't halt the Specials' demise. At their Top of the Pops appearance, Neville Staples, Terry Hall and Lynval Golding announced that they were leaving the group. "We didn't talk to the rest of the guys. We couldn't even stay in the same dressing room. We couldn't even look at each other. We stopped communicating. You only realise what a genius Jerry was years later. At the time, we were on a different planet", said Lynval.

"After more or less getting on my knees & begging them to do the song, I thought, after it got to # 1, 'I've proved myself to the band, they're going to respect me and realise that I knew what I was doing'. Critical acclaim, popularity, it's at number one, the critics think it's the best thing since sliced bread. Then Neville came into the dressing room & announced that they were leaving. I was really, really upset", said Dammers.

Roddy Byers quickly followed, who later played with Two Tone revival band, The Allstars. "I was relieved more than anything. If we'd carried on, I'd have ended up dead, or someone would've got hurt. I wish I hadn't drunk as much and argued less, but you can't change the way you are". Alienated by his involvement in Exegesis, Horace departed the following year: "I hated leaving. I just felt like I was being sucked into a black hole of depression. I was full of Exegesis and self-assertion & Jerry was dead against that. It must've been hell for him".

Dammers and drummer John Bradbury struggled to make a 3rd album, In the Studio, with new musicians. Released during 1984, it produced the hit single Free Nelson Mandela, leading Jerry to form Artists Against Apartheid, but otherwise its dark, foreboding songs about war, agoraphobia & racism sank without trace. "The Specials were a really unique combination of people. To find that kind of combination, the balance of the different folk, the different talents, it just doesn't come up very often", said Dammers.

It seemed inconceivable that a record with the musical and lyrical content of Ghost Town would get anywhere near the charts, much less make number one, Billy Bragg believing that it was a product of its time. "1981 was really one of those cusp years. It was the end of punk, but it was also the beginning of a more engaged politics of the '80s as a response to Thatcherism. 1981 was the year that Glastonbury was revived as a CND-supporting festival. Ghost Town wasn't just the end of everything, it also marked the beginning of something different. That built up to the miners' strike then Red Wedge in 1987, but we went out of fashion around the same time Margaret Thatcher went out of fashion. The demise of Thatcherism & the events that led up to the fall of the Soviet Union have left us in a post-ideological political landscape. It would be very difficult for young groups to make political music these days".

Jerry was still a musician, but had issued only a handful of records since the Specials' demise. "It does depress me that British music seems to have gone back to the way it was before punk. All these bands that sound like Gerry Rafferty, dressed up in trendy young people's outfits. It seems to have gone backwards, the music's split between black and white again. Some reggae guys once said to me, 'Ghost Town isn't the best record ever made by any means, but it's the best record ever to get to number one'".

It wasn't quite Blur vs Oasis for animosity, but the battle of The Specials v Busted was one of the most unlikely fights in pop history. Both had split at their height then faced years in the wilderness, although Terry Hall was less likely to form a splinter supergroup with McFly than the Year 3000 mob did with McBusted. Both were apparently getting on better than ever, each having released their comeback L.Ps at the start of Feb. '19. The Specials' magnificent Encore had beaten Busted's Half Way There by 1,060 sales, taking the ska survivors to the top of the album charts.

"Being at No.1? That's bonkers! The word 'cynical' isn't a nice one to use but when I first heard our record had made No.1, I thought, 'I'll believe it when I see it'. We did the best we possibly could with Encore and we're really proud of it but the response has been an awful lot more positive than I ever expected", stated the band's bassist Horace Panter.

It was just a coincidence that Encore arrived exactly a decade after The Specials played their 1st comeback shows, which were 28 years after they'd split up in the Top Of The Pops dressing room waiting to perform Ghost Town during 1981. However, the timing highlighted that one of the most important groups that Britain had ever produced were more in sync with each other than at any time in the 5 decades since they'd first formed as The Coventry Automatics in 1977.

It'd taken a decade for The Specials to issue 10 new songs, but Encore was the energetic opposite of a record borne out of careful planning. There wasn't a hint of cosiness in the L.P. from 3 men in their '60s, Terry, the baby of the group, having turned 60 on 19th March. "We're a dance band. How we approach our music is that we're a dance group with a message. Did then, do now", said singer/rhythm guitarist Lynval Golding.

Panter agreed, saying: "I wouldn't be doing my job properly if folk weren't dancing to our music. I'd be very upset if people aren't dancing to our album. It's what I still do in Coventry most weekends". The final word was left to relative newcomer Nikolaj Torp Larsen, the serene Danish keyboardist who'd been a Special since 2009, when Jerry Dammers was the sole founding member to skip the reunion: "The Specials audiences are great. If it grooves then they dance & if it doesn't groove, they start fighting. There's such adrenaline at Specials shows. If everyone is dancing, it's all good".

In the 38 years between Ghost Town and Encore, Horace had been a member of several Specials splinter bands. When Lynval, Terry and Neville Staple left to form Fun Boy Three, Panter stayed with Jerry & late drummer John Bradbury in The Special AKA. Other offshoots followed, with Horace sticking around for Special Beat and X Specials, so he was in a better position than most to establish what it was about the core line-up of him, Lynval & Terry that made Encore the work of the real Specials again.

"I think it's that we're a lot more mature. Everyone in this project was facing the same way; there was no agenda. Nobody was out of their head, nobody was getting in anyone's face. It's like that sign said at the recording of We Are The World: 'Check your egos at the door'. That was one of the unsaid aspects of Encore, that everyone had the same purpose, which has been transmitted into the music. The cynical realist in me thought, 'This could go wrong at any minute' but it didn't, it's been brilliant".

The antagonism of the original Specials that Panter alluded to peaked in the recording of their 2nd L.P. More Specials, Golding initially being wary of going into the studio at a Mitcham industrial estate where Encore was recorded over 4 weeks of the previous autumn. "The history of More Specials was that every day someone new would leave the band or threaten suicide. More Specials was always drama. This record? We were so relaxed! We never had a drop of alcohol in the sessions. That was amazing, as I'm from the old-school: 40 years of recording with a bottle of whisky, a bottle of gin, a 6-pack of lager. Encore? No alcohol. It was so enjoyable!"

Lynval and Nikolaj were in the HQ of the group's record label Universal, next to King's Cross station, where Horace came in a week later. Golding was itching to keep moving, a giant green beaded necklace bouncing as he spoke with the enthusiasm of someone living out an unlikely 2nd incarnation as what he called "Mr Big Pop Star". Relatively young at 45, Larsen was happy to let Lynval hold court – even when questions were addressed to him, soon deflecting them back to Lynval. Tall & slim, Nikolaj had the calm presence expected of someone who managed to get his 3 bandmates' disparate personalities flowing nicely while producing Encore.

Although Encore took a decade, the idea of a new Specials album had 1st surfaced during 2012. "We never had a long-term plan after we started in 2009, and we still don't," stated Panter, who'd been working for a decade as a teacher at Corley Centre when The Specials reformed, a school for children with communication difficulties in Warwickshire, combining that with working as a respected artist in the Pop Art field.

Horace spoke with a reasoned precision, occasionally saying "Does that make sense?" when he'd finished speaking. Panter still lived in Coventry, his accent coming through when he got excited, well fitting his nickname of Sir Horace Gentleman. Regarding Encore's genesis, he said: "When Lynval called me about the reunion, I thought: 'Shouting at children or being a rock star?' It was easy! I miss the children, but I don't miss the teaching. When we first started again, I thought: 'OK, we'll do this for a year then I'll go back to work as a teacher'. I figured I'd get to pay off my mortgage. It took off so well that we did it again during 2010 then again the following year but when it got to 2012 we thought, 'We should make a record'".

Before writing sessions could begin in earnest, 1st Neville Staple then guitarist Roddy Radiation left. Asked if either could come back, Golding replied: "Never say never. Where we are right now, we're enjoying this period. It's a wonderful time we're having. We've made some great songs & we're happy with that. Anything else? Time will tell". It was 2014 before writing began. Initially, The Specials played it safe, deciding which songs to cover for a new L.P.

"Rather than baring our souls straight away, we thought covers would be a good place to start – we were the original covers band anyway. We'd always taken an old song and recontextualised it. Monkey Man was initially about nightclub bouncers & we made it a comment on social unrest. We knew we had to acknowledge the past 40 years had happened, so we were listening to stuff like LCD Soundsystem. That's what we listened to for our version of The Equals' Black Skinned Blue Eyed Boys", Panter stated.

An audacious opening track, The Specials' update of the 1970 anti-war anthem by Eddy Grant's old group was a startlingly modern slice of disco. "When I first came to England from Jamaica in 1964, The Rolling Stones were my favourites. Then I saw The Equals on Top Of The Pops and that was it. Them being the first multi-racial band I'd seen, they made it seem so natural. People think 2 Tone was the time that music became multi-racial & right now feels a wonderful time to educate folk about The Equals getting there first", recalled Lynval.

The Valentines' early reggae classic Blam Blam Fever (1967) was another covered by The Specials', thick with hyperactive menace. "That's from touring a lot in America. I was fascinated by their gun culture, how you can buy guns in sports shops. It highlights America's gun crime, especially those hideous school shootings", said Horace.

Although lyrically still very relevant, perhaps the most surprising cover on Encore was The Lunatics (Have Taken Over The Asylum) the debut single of Fun Boy Three, issued just 5 months after they'd walked out on The Specials. There were rumours that it'd originally been planned as The Specials' single to follow Ghost Town. "I don't know whether we'd have gone ahead with it as a single, but yes, it was written while Terry, Lynval and Neville were still in The Specials. They were considering presenting it to the band, but then thought, 'Actually, we're probably better doing this on our own'", said Panter.

Mention of Fun Boy Three brought a big sigh from Golding. "Yes, it's true The Lunatics could've followed Ghost Town in The Specials, but everything got overtaken." A big pause. We were so big when Ghost Town came out, we could've been as mega as U2. Man, what a crazy band we were. We chose not to carry on down that road, because... I still wonder why we left to form Fun Boy Three. The Lunatics (Have Taken Over The Asylum) says a lot about us, too!"

Before Neville Staple left The Specials during 2013, there was vague talk about him, Lynval and Terry playing some Fun Boy Three concerts. "It crossed our mind," shrugs Lynval. "The difference is, The Specials is in our blood. Fun Boy Three did some nice things. Terry & I had become very creative, 'Faith,

Hope And Charity' is a great song. I'm proud of what Fun Boy Three did but can you imagine us and Bananarama with ra-ra skirts now?" asked Lynval

He & Horace both thought that taking some time off could've kept The Specials together longer. "It was intense. We had to ride that beast all the time & we got pulled forward and back by it. A little breather, it couldn't have hurt", said Golding. "More time off would've helped, but folk would've left anyway. We were all starting to find our own feet musically. A core might have remained, but not everyone", added Panter.

The Specials' reunion tours were a reminder of how powerful a live presence they were. It was those early touring days that were their fondest memories of their 1st incarnation, Horace recalling playing their first ever festival, in Belgium in August 1979, going on stage at 2pm after The Cure. "We'd had the same equipment for a couple of years, it was falling to bits. We had no roadies, we had to set everything up ourselves. Then we went on & we absolutely destroyed the place. There was a 12ft chain-link fence at the front of the stage. The audience tore it down, came charging towards the lip of the stage. It was the only time when I honestly felt that I could walk on water – and our music had done that. I realised, 'This is what our music can do'".

Powerful as the group were, their defiant politics & multi-racial line-up made them plenty of enemies. Why?, the B-side of Ghost Town, was recorded after Lynval was attacked by National Front thugs following a show during 1980, stabbed in the neck, being left with a small, vivid scar. Pointing at his neck he said "The scars went much deeper than this. It made me so scared for so long. I was in intensive care, but I was on so much pain medication that I couldn't feel anything. I heard a nurse say, 'We can't stop the bleeding'. I could see blood pouring out of me, but I thought, 'What are you talking about? I can't feel no blood!'

What happened hit me much later. Going out to a bar, I'd have my back to the wall, looking round everywhere to see if anyone wanted to stab me". Golding, appalled by the rise in knife crime, tapped his head. "I survived what happened, but in here it took me a long time to get over the emotional trauma. When I see reports of kids getting stabbed, I think of how long that pain really lasts".

One of the highlights of Encore was B.L.M. (Black Lives Matter), lyrically a companion to Why?, epic funk in the vein of Daft Punk's Giorgio By Moroder in which Lynval recounted his experiences of racism since he arrived from Jamaica at the age of 8 to live with his dad in Gloucester, who'd settled in England in the early '50s. They moved to Coventry 5 years later. "My father was invited by Sir Winston Churchill to rebuild England after the war. He'd been a tailor in Jamaica, but he couldn't get work at Burton the tailors in England, so he ended up in a foundry. He had to sleep in a garage", stated Golding.

Lynval's early experience of racism from fellow pupils in Gloucester were puzzling. "There were 3 white kids in my school in Jamaica. It was partly from the colonial system, but we were conditioned to look after the white minority kids. I thought a minority kid like me would get looked after too, so when kids yelled, 'Hey, you bl*ck b*stard!', I was terrified. It was completely alien to me". Having lived with his wife June in the US for over 20 years, Golding thought that social media was helpful in combating racism, saying: "Kids are getting killed by police brutality. Social media is brilliant for sharing images of that brutality, which would otherwise never get seen. It's where B.L.M. comes from".

As fine as his lyrics were on Encore, Hall had been reluctant to write for a new Specials album. "Terry is like one of those old cars with a crankshaft. You have to craaank Terry up to get his lyrics started. Thank God we did, because he's been amazing", said Lynval. Panter stated that it was only since the band had reformed that he'd become friends with their singer: "I don't think I ever knew Terry back in the day. There were 7 of us, so that's a lot of people to get to know. Now, I know that Terry is very, very funny".

Another reason that Encore had taken a long time was the impact of John Bradbury's passing during 2015. The drummer had been a key part of their early writing sessions, Golding recalling the pair of them threatening to kidnap Hall until he began writing songs again. Horace said: "Brad's death is something I might have suppressed, because it wasn't that difficult for me to play again without him. It was horribly unfortunate, of course, but you've got 2 choices – you carry on or you don't, and if it had been me that passed I'd have expected the guys to carry on".

Lynval had seen John the day before his death, when they watched Chelsea lose 3-0 to Terry's team Man. Utd. "We grumbled about what a woeful game it was then it was, 'OK, see you tomorrow', but Brad passed that day. It hit me like a ton of bricks. I couldn't breathe, hyperventilating because I'd been the last one in the band to talk to him. I've been on anti-depressants ever since".

John's drum stool was occupied by Kenrick Rowe, a friend of Nikolaj Larsen's who'd played with Mikey Dread & PJ Harvey. Larsen joined after playing keyboards for singer-songwriter James Morrison, being spotted by Lynval's friend Gareth Brown, Lily Allen's drummer. "The reason The Specials were apart for so long is that they had to wait for me to grow up then join them", joked Nikolaj, Golding adding: "It's true, we had to wait for this beautiful boy to get big".

Panter's appreciation of Larsen's skills was more practical, saying: "He has a musical virtuosity that Lynval and I don't possess. He has the arranger's talent that Jerry had, too. I made a big sign for the studio when we were recording that said 'Does it need it?' I'm very much in favour of minimal 4-track recording, whereas Nikolaj likes the kitchen sink. That balance is how Encore works".

Dammers' talent for arranging was a big part of The Specials' first line-up, only having been prepared to take part in a reunion if the songs were completely reworked, which was asking too much for the rest of the group. Lynval & Horace were sad rather than angry at their old bandmate, the latter saying: "I think about Jerry every day. It's a real shame that we couldn't resolve our differences, because we'd have made some fantastic music again. Could he still rejoin? In this business, never say never… he said diplomatically!"

Golding added: "I'll always have a special place in my heart for Jerry. It's tough to reflect on the past, because I think, 'Man, Jerry should be here with us', but we had to think about the audience. They want these songs the way they sounded. Jerry is a very talented man, but he was a little too far ahead of how we wanted to perform our songs".

can also feel the medication blocking it. It's brilliant! Recognising you're blocking it is amazing. It's really weird. It's like looking at a bruise develop on your leg".

The L.P's final track, We Sell Hope, was uplifting musically & lyrically, in contrast to the excoriation that came earlier. "Well, in the end, if you're talking about each other, all you can offer is love. To respect folk, be kind to people, and hope that they give it back. They sometimes don't but they sometimes do. There's that sense of hope. What else have we got?"

Gurinder Chadha (Film director) 'What moment from the height of your fame are you most proud of, the moment that provided the legacy of the Specials for years to come?"

HP: "Ghost Town getting to No 1".

TH: "Yes, I'd go with that. It was an unbelievably brilliant finale to what we'd done for a few years, and every band should fold after Ghost Town really, because what else are you going to do?!"

Richard Curtis (Film director) "I remember going to see you in concert when you got c. 10 secs into Ghost Town before stopping dead, pointing at some guy in the crowd, saying: 'If we don't get those Nazis out of here we're not going on with this song' then waiting until they were removed. Am I imagining this? Did I dream it?"

TH: "It used to happen every night, didn't it?"

HP: "It wasn't that much of an occurrence but it did happen, I remember maybe a couple or 3 times when we stopped a show because of the NF".

TH: 'They'd be sieg heiling during the show. That doesn't really happen any more. The closest thing to that was in Nottingham in 2014, where somebody threw a bottle at Brad & I couldn't do anything until he'd been taken out. It's important to stop stuff if you see it".

Joe Talbot (Lead singer, Idles) "Is pop much worse now than during the early '80s or am I blinded with nostalgia? Now it seems really dull when we glance at the mainstream".

TH: "I'm going to see Joe in a couple of weeks, his group. I don't know. We get asked that a lot. 'What're you listening to now?' What I'm listening to now is a Grateful Dead album, because I never heard it 1st time around".

HP: "I'm sure there are some things that are great out there but I don't know where to look for them. I haven't got the time to spend a fruitless 3 hrs ploughing through YouTube".

TH: "The last thing that I saw that I really, really liked was the Fat White Family. They were funny, everything you wanted. Bit druggy, funny, they look really good".

LG: "There's one band that I like. Easy Life. They're a young group from Leicester, I saw them on Jools Holland, they're really, really good. If I could have a vote for a band to be with us on any bill, it would be that little group. The kid's got the right attitude. He's a star".

Lauren Laverne (Music presenter) "When are you happiest?"

HP: "Most of the time".

LG: "With me, when we made the L.P., to get up, get on a train to go to work every day, go to the studio, that was really weird – but when we finished the record, I was completely lost. I didn't know what to do with myself. We had so much fun making this record. We'd take it in turns to sleep on the couch. 'Wake up', 'Oh, that's nice, yes', then go back to sleep".

TH: "Probably happiest when I'm watching football. Even through all the sh*tty times, 5 mins before kick-off you think: 'This is great', but in the last week or 2 do you know what's made me happiest? In our bathroom, on the floor there are mosaic tiles and one was lost. It's white, so I tried putting Polyfilla in, but I couldn't get the grouting to look good. Then I thought: 'Well, why don't I look in the vac bag?' so I got the bag out, put my hand in then found the tile. Honestly, that made me really happy. A great moment".

Richard Russell (Head of XL Recordings) "For Terry. You're one of my favourite lyricists of all time. Who're yours?'

TH: "Joe Dolce [Shaddap You Face]! No, obviously folk like Leonard Cohen, bits of Jeff Buckley & almost all Daniel Johnson and the Roches".

Ady Suleiman (Singer) "What're your best memories of 2 Tone?"

HP: "The Bilzen rock festival in Belgium during the summer of '79. We'd just signed our record deal with Chrysalis, we were unknown & we still had all this equipment that we'd begged, borrowed and stolen. We were on a bill with the Cure, the Pretenders, the Police and AC/DC. Nobody had heard of us but we went on stage then just destroyed the place. There was a big fence, 12 ft in front of the stage & during the performance it got ripped down then everyone surged to the front of the stage. For me, that was the most amazing experience ever, that music could do that was incredible".

TH: "Because of bands like UB40 and the Beat too, we were doing something that wasn't in London. It was a sense of pride in where we were & wanted to make some sort of change. Lyrically, I think what we were doing was all very similar. We were all in the Midlands, and the only band that I remembered from the Midlands was Jigsaw, who blew it all sky high".

LG: "Lieutenant Pigeon".

TH: "Frank Ifield. All of a sudden, something was happening, kids were connecting with us & it just felt really important".

Diane Morgan (Actress) "You wrote a song about a Ghost Town, but have any of you actually seen a ghost?"

LG: "I was born in Saint Catherine, Jamaica".

TH: "And he's off...".

LG: "This man was crippled, he sat in front of this house in the village where I come from, this brownstone house, on a mat. He died then I went down to the river with my sink pan on my head to fetch the water. It was broad daylight. I've got the water, I'm walking, then suddenly there he was, sitting in front of his house on his little mat. My mind just went, 'Wooah, wooah' & the sink pan of water has gone off my head. I just run and often now, I don't believe that I saw him, but I saw him. I still can't grasp it".

TH: "Weed's a funny thing, isn't it? I definitely haven't seen a ghost, no".

Jason Williamson (Singer, Sleaford Mods) "One thing that I find with accomplishment is that it can feel so insignificant overall, but I know that's something to do with bouts of depression. Do you feel this sometimes about what you've done & still do as musicians?"

TH: "It does matter, really, and even when it doesn't matter, it still matters. Folk see success as getting to No 1 & going platinum. I don't see that at all, I never have. I think the success is getting something inside, out, and getting someone to listen to it. That is success. For the first 20 years of my life, nobody would listen to me. Nobody. At school, jobcentres, they just didn't listen, they were never bothered but then you say something & somebody says, 'I agree, I disagree', so wow, somebody's listened! That's success".

Lee G. "Which song do you still love banging out the most?"

LG: "I like Nite Klub. It's a bit of a naughty one: 'I won't dance in a club like this/ All the girls are slags/ And the beer tastes just like piss'. It's what we guys, when we get together, we talk about. We don't shout it out loud to people. I quite enjoy that".

HP: "Yes, I'll go Nite Klub too. There's a version of it on the deluxe edition of the album, it's fantastic, I like it".

TH: "I quite like stuff from the 2nd L.P. International Jet Set & Stereotype. Just because I've always had this thing about folk seeing us as a ska group. We don't play ska music, and if you look at International Jet Set, you couldn't be more removed from ska. On the 2nd album, I couldn't pick one song, but I could say with that record: 'Wow, something good is happening here' then we split up!"

Angelina J. "I remember hearing Gangsters for the first time in 1979 when I was in an amusement arcade on my school holidays. The energy of that song stopped me in my tracks & the Specials have been my band ever since. What's your music moment that's stayed with you?"

TH: "I'd go with Gangsters, when we did it on Saturday Night Live in New York, because it felt so alien to the folk on the show, the ones working there and the audience & that was the 1st time that I thought: 'Something good's happening here'. We took off the shackles when we did it, people were just roaming on and off stage & it felt really like the right song at the right time. I remember doing photo sessions and folk thinking we were like a gay choir, because we all had short hair. Either ex-marines or a gay choir".

LG: "Remember when we did it in Chicago? When they got the audience to throw these fake dollar bills on the stage? Because… gangster, yes?"

TH: "Al Capone".

Miranda S.: "Can you think of a song that isn't yours where you thought: this changes everything?"

HP: "I was delivering car spares to a store in Birmingham. This was c. 1990., when this song came on the radio & I was standing there with this box, and this bloke was going, 'Come on, give me the box'. I go, 'Shh'. It was Smells Like Teen Spirit by Nirvana. It was the first time I heard it & I thought, 'Flippin' heck. That's good'".

LG: "'Get up, stand up. Stand up for your rights' by Bob Marley, because it was around the time when we started having our own identity. We started getting away from the colonial ways that were forced on to us and that's when the Rasta theme started coming up, something we could call our own. That really hit me".

Miranda S.: "How about you, Terry? Is there a song you can think of that changed things for you?"

TH: "I will come back to Shaddap You Face again… No, Anarchy in the UK. It was like everybody was waiting for something like that. It was a turning point".

Steve E. "If someone had told me 40 yrs ago that a bloke like [pro-Brexit 'yellow vest' protester] James Goddard & his mates would be close to the profile they have today, I would've found it hard to believe. You played a leadership role then. What do you think needs to happen now? How do we reverse the division that people like Goddard look to exploit?"

LG: "Back when we started, it was a small minority of skinheads that were pulling the wrong way. I remember one guy I met, a real National Front supporter, after I finished talking to him, we shook hands then we looked at each other & he said that he hadn't talked to a black guy before. He wouldn't do it but once we talked and had a discussion".

HP: "Those people always were out there. They feel more of a licence to speak now, because we all have our platform, don't we? This division is a knock-on effect of Instagram, Twitter & whatever. Everyone has a voice now but there's no filter on it. Back in our day, you would voice your discontent down the pub to your mates, whereas now you can voice your discontent to millions of folk from the privacy of your own downstairs toilet".

TH: "I think politicians love the division. It's a great thing for them. They thrive on it. I don't think they want everyone to be together. Brexit has conjured up so much stuff, and all these personalities are appearing, like Jacob Rees-Mogg. They like the division & I can see it getting a lot worse".

Stephen B. "Do you feel mellowed with age or do you still get intensely wound up by current political events?"

LG: "I switch on CNN then wonder: 'What am I watching all this for?' Folk calling the police because a little kid is selling water, just because the kid is black. The one thing which I think is good with social media is, when we say: 'You'll never understand what it's like to be black'. I think the images that come in now, you see it then maybe understand more. You walk in a shop and you know that all eyes are on you, because you appear like a guy who's going to come in to shoplift, because you're black... No, I'm not mellowed with age".

HP: "I think age has filtered a few things. The only thing I watch on TV is the news, really".

TH: "I've definitely mellowed but I'm at that age. I'm going to be 60 in a month & there's loads of sh*t going on, but then I look up at night, see the moon, and I just think: 'Whoa!' You see a tree that's been there a few hundred years then you think: 'F*cking hell. This is brilliant!'"

Miranda S.: "Was that age?"

TH: "No, it's medication. When you have kids of your own & with their mates, that's where you can be political and that's what I've tended to do, especially with my older boys when they were teenagers. Watching them go through stuff & hopefully guiding them. My house used to be a real open house, like a youth club. Their mates always used to come round, because I was like a bit 'right on', they could smoke weed or whatever and that's where you try to influence, so that there's not so much anger. It's not being mellow, you're doing something, but you're doing it at home, rather than just blasting it out all the time".

HP: "Micro as opposed to macro".

Liam N. "What're your thoughts on Coventry becoming a UK city of culture during 2021? Had they been approached to do something?"

HP: "I'm the only participating member of the Specials who still lives in Coventry, but no, I haven't been approached to do something. I'd like to see money put by to provide for music lessons for children in schools, a proper legacy. I'm more interested in that than 'Here's a couple of boutique hotels' & who needs another wine bar for goodness sake?"

TH: "I get really bugged by this City of Culture thing. If you have to really search for the culture, you're making it up. The landmark for me in Coventry is the cathedral".

FlightGuileAndPies "I'm a Cov kid, who grew up as all the industry collapsed around us in the '80s and '90s, losing perhaps 100,000 jobs in that time from Jaguar, Triumph, Dunlop, Rover, Rolls-Royce, Morris, Alvis, Massey Ferguson. I wonder how you see the city today with so many of those jobs replaced by call centres? People who had repetitive production line jobs at least had the pride of being part of making something that was known, in some cases worldwide. Now they just get shouted at by irate customers on the phone".

LG: "You used to have Courtaulds. They were everywhere. Massey Ferguson that does the tractors & in Canley, Matrix Churchill, one of the last pieces of work they were doing was making parts for arms for the Iraq war. Obviously that war game didn't work out for them, because war brings employment for them. It's all gone now. Even the smell of the city isn't there any more. You could smell the engineering. Back then, Coventry was thriving, an industrial city. Now it's a student city".

HP: "Loads of barbers".

LG: "And chicken shop takeaways. It's all revolving around students. Working class, labour folk – once the industry goes away then all the traditional pubs, they die. The working men's clubs, they die. Like what my father used to go to, Rowley's Green Working Men's Club. They're not there any more".

HP: "There's still manufacturing in Coventry".

LG: "You've got Triumph motorbikes".

HP: 'London taxis are made in Coventry".

TH: 'All my family worked in factories. My mum worked for Chrysler, my dad worked for Rolls- Royce. Aunt. Everybody worked in the car factories & there was a real sense of community. Everybody felt on an equal level, all getting cash every week. I didn't really notice the decline, really, until it had happened, but then it was massive. It's difficult with Coventry, because I moved away for specific reasons. I couldn't f*cking stand it".

Peter M. "What was it like touring with the Clash?"

LG: "It was absolutely an eye-opener. Joe Strummer was a wonderful, wonderful human being, and being in that group of people at that time, there was so much excitement. Because we did our little pub thing, but this was like the next level up. It was just a wonderful vibe. Like one big party".

HP: "We learned how to present a show while on tour with the Clash. You'd see how they went on stage & it was just like, Bang. We learned to give 100%. Not just shamble on stage and 'If you don't mind, we'd like to play a few songs'. We were totally different after that tour. I always say that we started that tour as civilians but ended it as a group".

TH: After the Clash thing, that's when we cut our hair, because we discovered what we should look like by doing that tour. Then you end up in Crawley with c. 1,000 skinheads gobbing at you".

HP: "That was scary".

TH: "Yes, that was really scary but it was great, because Suicide were on that tour as well & Sham did stuff. Jimmy Pursey was there. For me, it was like, 'How do you react to an audience?' The fans tell you the songs they like. They like Monkey Man, definitely and A Message to You, around the world".

Barry M. "I heard that activist Saffiyah Khan has sung on the L.P. How had that come about?

TH: "We saw Saffiyah in that photo. She had a Specials T-shirt on & she was standing up to a member of the English Defence League, who was screaming at her, she just smiled back. A fantastic reaction, because it made him look stupid. So we got in touch with her to say: 'Come to our gig in Birmingham'. Then when it came to recording the album, we were thinking about folk who might like to be on it, and she was definitely in my head as somebody who could have something to say. At the same time I was listening to Prince Buster, Ten Commandments of Man & I couldn't believe...".

Miranda S.: "How rampantly sexist it is?"

TH: "It goes back to DLT, like hand-on-the-arse times. So then the idea came like: 'Wouldn't it be nice to do an answer to that?' but obviously from a woman. Saffiyah was the obvious choice, and we just said to her: 'Here's the Prince Buster song. Do you want to try to reply to it?' then she got on with it".

Tenement F. "Bloody hell, I don't think I've seen such effortlessly cool looking gentlemen ever. Please give me a clothing tip".

HP: "Smart casual, wear your T-shirt outside your jeans".

LG: "Horace is stepping up now, he's the man. Me, I like that sort of stuff from the '70s, like reggae style. Gregory Isaacs".

TH: "It's simple. Avoid horizontal stripes. Didn't work when you were 18 mate & now you're middle aged".

Thehumblegent "Terry, as a lifelong Man Utd fan, what do you think Ole Gunnar Solskjær has to do to get the manager's job full time?"

TH: "No idea what he has to do. I mean, he just wins at the moment. He's such a lovable bloke and a real legend, but whether he'll keep the job, who knows?"

LG: "He's a real Man U guy, he spent half his life there, it's in his blood & it's got to be in your blood to be able to manage a club like that. I think they should hold on to him, give him the job full time. It could be another Fergie in the making".

TH: "I think realistically, for me, Ferguson is managing the club again. He's using Solskjær as his mouthpiece. Ferguson is smiling way too much".

LG: "It's brilliant. The next legend manager".

Bloodydoorsoff "Now you're doing new material like Jerry wanted to do when you reformed, isn't it time to let him back into the fold?"

HP: "No. Next question".

LG: "I think having Nikolaj Torp Larsen, we're really fortunate to have a kid like that who's so talented. I was one of the last ones to work with Jerry, I enjoyed working with him. If you're going to make music, you want to make music with folk that you respect as musicians. I do respect him a lot".

TH: "The whole Jerry thing, it's like, from day one, I'm not sure why he isn't in the group. I honestly don't know, because we all started rehearsing together [for the 2009 reunion] but he sort of dropped out. I don't know what happened there. I don't know why he isn't in the band. He just, dropped out. It's his stuff really, it's not our stuff. He chose not to be in the group, for whatever reasons".

Miranda S.: "What about if he asked: 'Oh, can I come back?'"

TH: "I'd just tell him to f*ck off. No, I wouldn't, I'd get management to tell him. He can come back, it's up to him what he's going to do".

Diesel Estate "Why weren't Neville, Roddy and Jerry back in the band?"

HP: "They left".

LG: "They left. It's as simple as that. Roddy left the group, Neville left the band. Jerry didn't fully join the group back. There's nothing we can do about it".

TH: "Roddy & Neville feel comfortable where they're at. They play pubs & small clubs, and I think if you lack that much charisma then that's probably a wise thing. They enjoy small intimate venues with very few people there. That's where they feel most comfortable".

Sam McN. "For Terry and Horace. What does painting do for you that making music doesn't?"

TH: "When I was at my ill-est, it triggered something in my brain that wouldn't allow me to talk or walk for 3 weeks. Because I couldn't say anything, I had to write everything down & a doctor said to me: 'Paint'. Actually painting was something that was coming out of my head that I could show to folk. For them, in Horace's case, to despise".

Miranda S.: "It's a reaction".

TH: "I've got a fixation on the Jackson 5, so I painted the Jackson 5 for 6 months then it was pointed out to me that I'd painted 6. Six Jacksons, so I renamed the extra one Phil Jackson. It's all getting it out, and who cares whether it's right or wrong, I don't give a sh*t".

HP: "Music for me is a collaborative process, I'm a bass player. I have to work with a drummer, a singer, a keyboard player, I'm a cog in a machine. The art is kind of my solo album".

The Specials flew to New York to make their US television debut during June 1980, performing their first single, Gangsters on Saturday Night Live. To the wave of American ska-punk bands who appeared in the mid'90s, The Specials appearance had become legendary, the stuff of hushed, reverential tones & fuzzy, nth-generation video copies passed among collectors. For the members of Rancid and No Doubt at least, it was a perfect, inspirational moment: The Beatles on Ed Sullivan in Sta-prest & a pork pie.

However, for The Specials the memory was different. Weary from touring, they argued about their hotel, about the limo NBC sent to take them to the studio, about what they should do on the show. Jerry Dammers, the group's leader and troubled political conscience, thought the hotel was too flash & expensive, the limo was just rock-star bollocks, the live show was a platform to say anything that the band really wanted to say. The others disagreed. "Jerry was thinking so far ahead of us. He said to us, 'It's a live TV show in front of millions of people, we can do anything we want'. I just thought, Oh my God, he's really lost it. We're dealing with racism & political problems in England and he wants to take on America as well", recalled Lynval Golding.

They played a tense, speedy version of Gangsters instead: wrestling with their instruments, no eye contact except the occasional glower. On the one hand, it's an incredible performance: a splenetic, wild burst of energy set to ferocious, groundbreaking, thrilling music. On the other, something's clearly very wrong with the people on stage. Grim faces, their movements are slightly too aggressive. The band seems barely in control of what's going on. At any moment you feel the whole thing could prematurely collapse & this lot could start punching each other.

Viewing their performance was rather like seeing The Specials career condensed into 2 1/2 mins. As Jerry Dammers surmised a couple of decades after the group folded: "It was a laugh to start off with, it was great but it ended in chaos, total chaos". Jerry first met Roddy Byers in the early '70s, before the latter changed his name to become Roddy Radiation. "I was c. 15, the first band I had was called Gristle. I played the drums. Just recently I was reading this interview with Roddy and it turns out he was in that group. It only clicked this year that it was the same guy: he had long hair at that stage & I just didn't remember. Anyway, he was telling the story and he said, 'Jerry's band had this weird name: Rissole'. Maybe our communication problems stemmed from then", stated Dammers.

The son of a Coventry clergyman, Jerry had other musical plans. A fellow student at Lanchester Polytechnic, Horace Panter, remembered "this weird looking bloke with tartan trousers, who used to smash things up". While Panter played bass in a soul band, Dammers became part of "a small group who dressed like teds or skinheads. We used to wreck the hippie parties, play Prince Buster records. I had this band playing dodgy versions of Desmond Dekker's 007. We used to gob at each other on stage. It was like a forerunner of punk".

After college, there was a brief period with New Faces winning covers group Sissy Stone then Jerry asked Horace to help him record some of his songs. They were joined by a vocalist called Tim Strickland, "A kind of Lou Reed chap, he didn't really sing, he sort of glowered & spat", remembered Panter, along with a couple of refugees form Coventry's multiracial soul scene: a Barbadian drummer called Silverton Hutchinson and Jamaican guitarist Lynval Golding. Christened The Coventry Automatics, the quintet muddled through Dammers songs. "I used to have reggae lessons. Lynval used to come round my flat, play records & go, 'Listen, mon! De bass should sound like dis! I got the hang of it eventually", recalled Horace.

They got a residency at a club called Mr Georges - 40p to see the band support Coventry's punk combos. One punk group, Squad, yielded their 17-yr-old lead singer to replace Tim Strickland in The Automatics. Terry Hall often performed with his back to the audience. "He worked in a stamp shop. I told him, Philately will get you nowhere'", said Jerry. Despite Terry's off stage shyness and youth - 5 yrs younger than Dammers - he was a remarkably capable front man. "If anybody in the audience fought, Terry had a great way of putting them down. He'd pick them out then ask the rest of the audience what they thought of them, just make them feel completely small", said Roddy Byers.

Hall thought that his abilities had less to do with stage craft than his exercises on Coventry's streets: "Me & Roddy were in the 1st bands of punks that ever appeared in Coventry and the people took the piss all the time. That only made us more hardened to ridicule, so afterwards things didn't worry us again". However, Panter thought that he was an aloof presence in the group: "I don't ever remember saying much to Terry".

The Automatics attracted the attention of DJ Peter Waterman, famed for playing Philly soul at Coventry's Locarno with Neville & The Boys, a dance troupe featuring roadie Neville Staple. Waterman offered The Automatics time in Soho's Berwick Street Studios. Looking to flesh out their sound, and unaware of their shared history, Jerry invited his former Gristle/Rissole band mate, Roddy Byers, to join.

Byers came complete with his own anthem to urban alienation, Concrete Jungle, but if the appointment of a punk guitarist was intended to smooth out the group's lumpy attempts to fuse punk & reggae, it failed. In Berwick Street, they lurched gracelessly from one genre to another. They were also sick of Peter's advice. "We had to get rid of him when he tried to teach Terry Hall to dance. He got on stage to demonstrate. It was unpleasant. It involved hip swinging", said Dammers.

Jerry looked for other routes to stardom. Through Steve Connolly, a Clash roadie, he blagged a meeting with Bernie Rhodes, Clash manager. He managed to talk his band, renamed The Special AKA The Automatics, onto the On Parole Tour of 1978. "Suicide were the official support but they couldn't make the 1st dates, so we were supposed to fill in for them. Then Neville started supplying Mick Jones weed, so we were allowed to stay. It was like being in a film. It was ace", said Horace.

The tour was the making of The Specials. Neville Staple became a member after plugging a microphone into the mixing desk at London's Music Machine then toasting along with the group's set. Skinheads disrupted the tour in Bracknell, the National Front, in political decline due to losing votes to the Tories, having shifted tactics, recruiting football hooligans and skinheads.

"That was the night The Specials concept was born. It was obvious that the Mod/skinhead revival was coming & I was trying to find a way to make sure it didn't go the way of the NF. I idealistically thought, 'We have to get through to these people', and that's when we got the image together & started using ska rather than reggae. It seemed a bit more healthy to have an integrated kind of British music, rather than white folk playing the 2. During the '40s - '50s, Professor Longhair took on board Caribbean rhythms then Jamaica picked up on New Orleans sound. You got Afro-Cuban jazz combining North American jazz with African rhythms - and that's the roots of ska", said Dammers.

There were also less idealistic reasons for the band's new image. "We looked odd. I was this sort of Woolworth's skinhead, Terry wore loud checked jackets & Jerry had tartan trousers. We saw the mod revival thing going on and you could still buy tonic suits in Gosford Street real cheap," stated Panter. Rhodes kindly allowed The Special AKA to move into The Clash's rehearsal studios in Chalk Farm, north London. "It was freezing. Sleeping on the floor, rats jumping over you", remembered Golding.

Bernie booked them a gig in Paris, the trip becoming part of Specials legend. At Dover, their driver told them to unload the van then drove off. Silverton Hutchinson was refused entry to France because of his Barbadian passport. The van that picked up them up was only big enough for 2 members, so Neville and Lynval got in while the others hitched. At their hotel the management complained that the last English group to stay there, The Damned, had smashed the place up, snatching Golding & Byers guitars in lieu of payment. "There was a lot of shoving in the hotel lobby then the manager of the club turned up and told us to go to the club. By the time we arrived our guitars were there", Lynval related. "We thought, 'How did they do that?' Then the manager of the club arrived, he offered me & Terry a mint. As he opened his jacket, we saw a gun", said Roddy.

The trip led to the demise of both Bernie Rhodes as manager and Silverton as drummer, the latter being unsure about the shift to ska & fed up living in penury. "He walked into the rehearsal one day, called us a bunch of wankers then left", recalled Golding. Back in Coventry, they borrowed money to fund a recording session, featuring Dammers' flatmate John Bradbury on drums.

Inspired by Stiff and Rough trade, 1979 was the year of the indie label: hundreds of hopeful bands began their own cottage industries, Jerry's among them. He designed the 2 Tone label, with its black and white checks & 'rude boy' mascot, Walt Jabsco, whose name came from a 2nd hand bowling shirt, his image being a crudely drawn copy of an early photo of Peter Tosh. "The Wailers trying to be The Impressions. The 2 Tone man was an impression of an impression of The Impressions", said Dammers.

Backed by The Selecter, an instrumental recorded in 1977 by John Bradbury and guitarist Neol Davies, Gangsters riff was borrowed from Prince Buster's Al Capone, changing the inaugural cry to 'Bernie Rhodes knows, don't argue!' & the band's Parisian experience: 'Don't interrupt while I'm talking or I'll confiscate all your guitars'. Recognisably post-punk because of Terry Halls' monotone vocal, yet danceable as '60s ska, it sold steadily for 6 months, helped by John Peel's plays and the group's live reputation. By May, when the Special AKA played the Fulham Greyhound, Mick Jagger was in the audience, keen to sign them to Rolling Stones Records. Horace said that he left the gig in a huff because of the similarity of the band's Little Bitch to Brown Sugar.

The Specials signed to Chrysalis, in a deal brokered by their new manager, Rick Rogers, a former associate of The Damned. "Chrysalis was more open than anyone to the idea of the 2 Tone label, which was sort of groundbreaking. Mind you, they were laughing all the way, because they got the talent spotting and A&R done for nothing", said Jerry. The Specials picked up momentum at remarkable pace. Uniquely in the post punk landscape they were a complete, easily accessible package: a 'new' sound, an image, a political stance and an hyperactive live show.

"You get this fantastic feeling of togetherness playing ska, because no one individual could do it on their own. It all interlocks - you get this communal feeling between the musicians onstage & that spreads into the audience like a fever. That's why The Specials gigs and the 2 Tone gigs were the wildest the country has ever seen. They were just absolutely f*cking incredible", stated Dammers.

Gangsters was in the Top 10 & on Top of The Pops by June 1979, where host Peter Powell introduced them "The Specials there. Good time music from Coventry". However, with the group's rise in popularity came the first signs of the tensions that would destroy them, Jerry being uncomfortable with his celebrity. "Everywhere you would go, everyone acts abnormal. 'He's in The Specials - act abnormal!' It's like entering The Twilight Zone or something. It can be a bit weird, to put it mildly, especially as it happened really quickly".

During the recording of their debut L.P., producer Elvis Costello was unimpressed by Byers' Clash influenced licks, unsuccessfully arguing that Jerry should sack him but it was the 1st step to the guitarist's gradual estrangement from Dammers. Like many debut albums, Specials was a thunderous run through the band's set, its live feel helped by Costello's thin production. While punk had been a phenomenon largely revolving around London - from the Clash's Westway strife to Sham 69's suburban bovver - The Specials were resolutely provincial. Terry Hall sang in a deadpan Midlands' monotone. Nite Klub was set in a shabby Coventry ballroom, where 'all the girls are slags and the beer tastes just like piss'.

Despite the presence of Jamaican ska trombonist Rico & its Toots and the Maytals covers, Specials was a L.P. concerned with the preoccupations of post punk British youth. The National Front was on the march; teds fight punk's bovver boys lurking around every corner waiting to put the boot in. Its release that October was heralded by the 2 Tone Tour of The Specials with Madness and The Selecter, which was marred by crowd violence.

"The amount of violence at specials gigs has been exaggerated down the years. I really wish there hadn't been any. The great majority were trouble free, but there were a few where a minority thought they were supposed to have a scrap. With c. 4 exceptions, any sign of trouble was nipped in the bud by the group stopping then Terry stating that it wasn't part of the deal", said Jerry. In Bristol, Neville Staple discovered that his fame meant that girls were willing to star with him in hotel room porn. On November 7th, all 3 bands appeared together on Top of The Pops. In just 3 months, 2 Tone had gone from indie label to a UK wide phenomenon.

"The Specials played 2 gigs in Coventry at Tiffany's that Christmas. That was the apogee of 2 Tone, for me. Coventry was an industrial motor city, lots of unemployment. Without being melodramatic, it raised folks spirits here a bit", said Panter. The group's punishing live schedule ensured that things would never truly be the same again. Buoyed by the speed of The Specials rise in England, their manager Rick Rogers was keen for the band to break America: a 6 week US tour was booked, followed by a lengthy European leg. From their arrival in America, it was clear that all wouldn't be going to plan.

"It's hard to believe now, but at the time, the concept of retro didn't exist in the US at all. We arrived at the airport in our tonic suits & pork pie hats, ready to take America by storm, but this bloke who picked us up in the minibus said to Rick, 'Say, are these guys mental patients?' He really thought we were from a mental hospital because of the suits and short hair", said Dammers.

The group ploughed on with a support slot for The Police then a headlining tour. In Los Angeles they were booked for 8 shows in 4 nights at the Whisky a Go Go. "It was one of the stupidest things that ever happened to The Specials. On stage we're putting everything in to it. Playing 2 shows / night was like putting someone in for 2 boxing matches / night - it made no sense at all. I hate to say it, but that really broke the spirit of the band. We were completely exhausted. After that, everybody stopped getting on", stated Jerry.

Even news from the UK that The Specials Live EP had topped the charts couldn't lift the group's mood. Dammers hadn't done much to endear himself to the US public by telling a press conference that he "could've had more fun on a school trip to Russia", while his insistence that the band turn down limousines & flashy hotel accommodation was irking at least one of his fellow Specials: "I was getting pissed off. Maybe he came from a background where he was privileged, but the rest of us didn't, so let's enjoy it a bit. You get a limousine sent, who wants to go in the van with the gear? F*ck that, I'm from the streets - let me live a bit', said Staple.

However, Jerry remained largely unrepentant: "Its' hard to discuss things with Neville - I wish I'd tried more. Maybe a vicar's pay was actually low enough to teach me some respect for money. We didn't travel in the van with the gear, we travelled in a normal tour bus and the hotels were fine, with a few exceptions. It seems odd now, because rock music has returned to excess, but durinh the early '80s it was different. I remember Bad Manners staying in a hotel where the lobby was made out of remnants. I got a train once with Dexys Midnight Runners & they all had to bunk the fare. You're buying into the American dream, you're buying into bullsh*t, and you're being flash with money. The amount of money that gets wasted on tour is phenomenal".

"It was fine in the beginning, but it became difficult when there was nothing left to rebel against. We couldn't sing about unemployment when we were buying ready meals for 2 at Marks & Spencer", said Terry Hall. On their return to England, Roddy's student baiting Rat Race became The Specials 4th successive Top 10 and Lynval Golding was attacked by racists outside Hampstead Moonlight Club. "I got beat up badly. My ribs were smashed in. It was a frightening experience. It was a racist attack, it was because I was walking down the road with 2 white girls", stated Lynval. The day after the attack he was given painkilling injections so that he could play the Montreux Jazz Festival.

The issue of The Specials drug use & its effect on their deteriorating relationships, was a thorny one. None of the ex-members agreed on exactly who was taking what. There was a lot of pot smoking - on the tour bus, trombonist Rico dispensed marijuana and wisdom from his ever-present Bible but Horace was adamant that after America "cocaine reared its ugly head". Others disputed that, but all agreed that alcohol was a destructive force within the group. "When everybody got sloshed & all that crap, I used to go back to the room with my weed and women. When they were pissed, that was when their inhibitions came out, that's when it all became 'I hate you'. I never thought, 'He's like that because he's been taking cocaine or amphetamines', I thought, 'He's is like that because he's been f*cking drinking'", said Neville.

Whatever the reasons, by the time The Specials embarked on their tour of British seaside resorts during the summer of 1980, relations in the band, especially between Dammers and Byers, both heavy drinkers, were strained to breaking point. Jerry's original idea was for the group to sail around Britain on a boat, anchor offshore then travel to the gigs by speedboat. "That got translated by our manager into doing a tour of every seaside town in Britain. That sort of thing happened often with Rick Rogers. His intentions were totally right but it somehow went wrong. For too long the group doubled up in hotel rooms because that was what we did in the early days & Rick thought that I didn't want the policy changed. Of course I did".

"On the 1st day of the tour, Jerry was going 'I don't want to do this'. Everybody else was saying 'The trucks are here, the tickets have been sold'. I suggested doing it with another keyboard player, because I could see that Jerry was at the end of his tether, but the rollercoaster had started - nobody was allowed to get off it", said Panter.

During a photo session on tour, an argument about clothes ended with Radiation nearly pushing Dammers over a cliff top, who said "Actually, Roddy give me one of those jokey little pushes, but it was a bit more dangerous that it should've been". Later that night, Byers smashed his guitar over Jerry's keyboard mid set, who didn't know what was wrong: "It wasn't as if anybody had told me what the problem was". "I always rebelled against authority and Jerry started to be an authority to me. I saw him as the guy who was telling me what I could & couldn't do. I wasn't happy with my internal situation (having briefly split from his wife) and I was drinking too much. I was being a total arsehole", Roddy later explained.

Ongoing sessions for the group's 2nd album were tense. "Every day someone left. It was horrible," said Golding. Dammers wanted to venture beyond the 1st L.P's ska roots, having become interested in muzak & easy listening, a dramatic shift in sound which led to some consternation in the band, Staple and Byers being particularly unimpressed. Chrysalis Records were nonplussed by Stereotype, a mournful dirge satirising lads culture earmarked as a single but despite its wilful uncommerciality, it hit UK # 6.

Other group members became resentful of Jerry's control. "Everybody was into different kinds of music, but Jerry still wanted to control what was happening. He'd been right up to that point, but I started to think he was losing it a bit. He wanted to use drum machines. I didn't want them on my songs", Roddy recalled.

Dammers responded: "I wanted everyone to write songs, I didn't want to do it all myself. Just trying to keep everyone happy was difficult. Roddy had a song called 'We're only monsters'. The lyrics went something like, 'We're not the boys next door, we're the werewolves from down your street'. It wasn't right for the album, so I told him to go write something else. He came back with this song with the lyrics essentially saying 'Jerry Dammers is a heartless bastard and he won't do any of my songs'. I was like, 'No, that's not a good one either'. Then Neville came up with this idea, called Neville's Erotic Sounds. It was ahead of its time, genius. It had classical music & dub reggae playing at the same time in the background and Neville arguing with some girl about having a tape recorder under the bed. I didn't like to listen much further than that".

Issued in September 1980, More Specials betrayed the atmosphere that surrounded its creation. Its music was brilliantly varied - leaping from reggae to Northern Soul to Jerry's jazz-inspired exotica - its tone inescapably bleak. International Jet Set despairingly examined the misery of touring. Terry's Man At C&A was rife with nuclear paranoia, while Pearl's Café, which dated back to the Coventry Automatics, matched jaunty ska to a bitter, frustrated chorus: 'It's all a load of bollocks and bollocks to it all'.

On the ensuing tour the fans' stage invasions had got out of control. "At first it was a great laugh - we're all in this together, there's no stars here. Then folk were getting on-stage 2 numbers into the set. It became tedious & dangerous, but you couldn't stop it. One gig we told the audience it was too dangerous but they wouldn't have it, so it ended up in a massive ruck with the bouncers", recalled Dammers.

An audience member jumped on-stage in Cambridge then attacked the support group, The Swinging Cats. Violence between bouncers and the audience flared throughout The Specials' set. Hall hurled a mic-stand at one bouncer. Jerry announced that the band would stop if the violence didn't cease but another bouncer got on-stage then threatened him. After the gig, Terry and Dammers were arrested at the behest of the promoter then charged with incitement to riot, being fined £400.

Hall, usually calm on-stage, was perturbed: "As a group we're now thinking whether or not to carry on doing tours. We don't like violence at our concerts, we've made that clear from the outset. We offer music as an alternative to fighting. It's easier to use your energy dancing than punching someone in the mouth. Anyway, if the fighting doesn't stop, there's only one way to make it stop, we either stop gigging or call it a day". "You're in this fantastic group making wonderful music but you can't play it anymore because folk are hitting each other. I ran away, I went to America after that tour. It became absolutely unbearable", said Horace.

Worn down by the pressures of life as a Special, Panter became involved in 'Exegesis', a religious cult that preached self-assertion, another celebrity adherent being Mike Oldfield. "Just to add to the fun &

games, Horace joins some nutty cult then starts giving them all his money! Anyone who knows anything about those cults and trying to get people out of them... it was a nightmare", stated Jerry.

The band reconvened in early 1981 to rehearse Dammers' epic Ghost Town, which had been inspired by scenes glimpsed during their previous tour. "In Liverpool, all the shops were shuttered up, everything was closing down. In Glasgow there were little old ladies on the streets selling all their household goods, their cups & saucers. It was clear something was very, very wrong".

The song's noble intent didn't make the rehearsals or recording sessions any easier. "People weren't co-operating at all, Every little bit of Ghost Town was worked out, all the different parts, it wasn't a jam session. I can remember walking out of rehearsals in total despair because Neville wouldn't co-operate. You know the brass bit is kind of jazzy, it has a dischord? I remember Lynval rushing into the control room while they were doing it going, 'Wrong! Wrong! Wrong!' In the meantime, Roddy's trying to kick holes in the studio wall. The engineer was going, 'If that doesn't stop, you're going to have to leave!' I was saying 'This is the greatest record that's ever been made in the history of anything! You can't stop now!'", said Dammers.

Ghost Town was a remarkable record, The Specials greatest achievement. Aside from its musical content - a doomy mesh of reggae rhythms, jazzy chord progressions and stabbing John Barry brass - there was the matter of its sheer prescience. As the track shot to the top of the charts during June 1981, its lyrical prediction - 'the people getting angry' - was chillingly borne out. Riots erupted in Brixton & Toxteth, Liverpool then spread around Britain's deprived inner cities. No record in British pop history has ever matched the news so accurately.

However, its success couldn't save The Specials. Despite telling the media that "The Specials as a working unit are stronger than ever, and I feel we've got a lot more to give", Terry had been working on demos with Lynval & Neville before the Ghost Town sessions. "It was just an idea as a break from the band, like Damon from Blur's done with Gorillaz but no one was talking, no communication in the group, we couldn't even look at each other", Golding later stated.

"After more or less getting on my knees and begging the band to do the song, I thought after it got to # 1 that I'd proved myself to the group, that they were going to realise that I knew what I was doing. We had popularity & critical acclaim. We got on Top Of The Pops then Neville came into the dressing room to announce that they were leaving. I was really, really upset", said Jerry.

Inevitably Byers also left. "I was relieved. If I'd carried on in the band, I'd have ended up dead or someone would've got hurt. I wish I'd drunk less and not argued so much, but you can't change the way you are". Dammers was determined to continue with Panter, Bradbury & singer Rhoda Dakar, who'd left Conference League 2 Toners The Bodysnatchers, bringing with her their sole original number, The Boiler. About an attempted rape climaxing in harrowing screams, it was the first single released by the new line-up, re-christened The Special AKA. It reached # 35 six months after Ghost Town topped the charts, indicating both that the single was deliberately uncommercial and 2 Tone's time had slipped away.

Jerry retreated to Coventry to search for new-musicians. "I had a lot of loyalty to Coventry, but the pool of talent wasn't big enough. John Shipley was from The Swinging Cats, Stan Campbell came in on vocals. It was out of the frying pan & into the fire really". Sessions for their 3rd L.P. lasted a fortnight before Horace quit, alienated by his continued involvement in Exegesis: "I could see that Jerry was struggling, but I was full of Exegesis and self-assertion & he was dead against that. It must've been hell for him. I hated leaving. I couldn't change Jerry's mind, make him go away for a bit, get some inspiration. He was going to confront it head-on."

The sessions lurched on. John Bradbury belatedly emerged as a songwriter, contributing a couple of tracks, but could see matters were spiralling out of control: "It took an inordinate amount of time. There didn't seem to be any rehearsals for it - it all took place in the studio. Did Jerry tell you how much it cost? It was loads. The money being spent was ridiculous. There was no way the album was going to recoup it unless it got to No. 1 and sold across the continents".

That clearly wasn't going to happen: their next single, War Crimes, with its awkward rhythm & lyric comparing Beirut to Belsen, was issued at Christmas 1982 but flopped. The similarly uncompromising Racist Friend stalled at # 60. Stan Campbell was unimpressed: he'd thought that he was joining a chart-topping combo. "It got a bit hairy at the end, that group. Nelson Mandela was the same as Ghost Town. I literally had to beg them to do it, which was really humiliating. I knew it was a really important song, but once again people didn't want to co-operate", said Dammers

It was the final track to be recorded for The Special AKA's 3rd album, prosaically named In The Studio, being its sole hit, with implications beyond it's chart placing, as had Ghost Town. "Jesus, it really woke folk up. A lot of people had never heard of the guy before that", said Bradbury. In The Studio flopped. "The record company did no promotion on it at all. I think they spent £9,000 on promotion, which considering all the time that had been spent on it was just ridiculous", argued Jerry. It was an ignoble fate for an underrated L.P., although how could a label market an album in 1984 that was filled with tricky time signatures and brooding songs about alcoholism & agoraphobia? "£9,000 on promotion? After Jerry had finished recording that's probably all the money the record company had left", joked John when reminded of the figure.

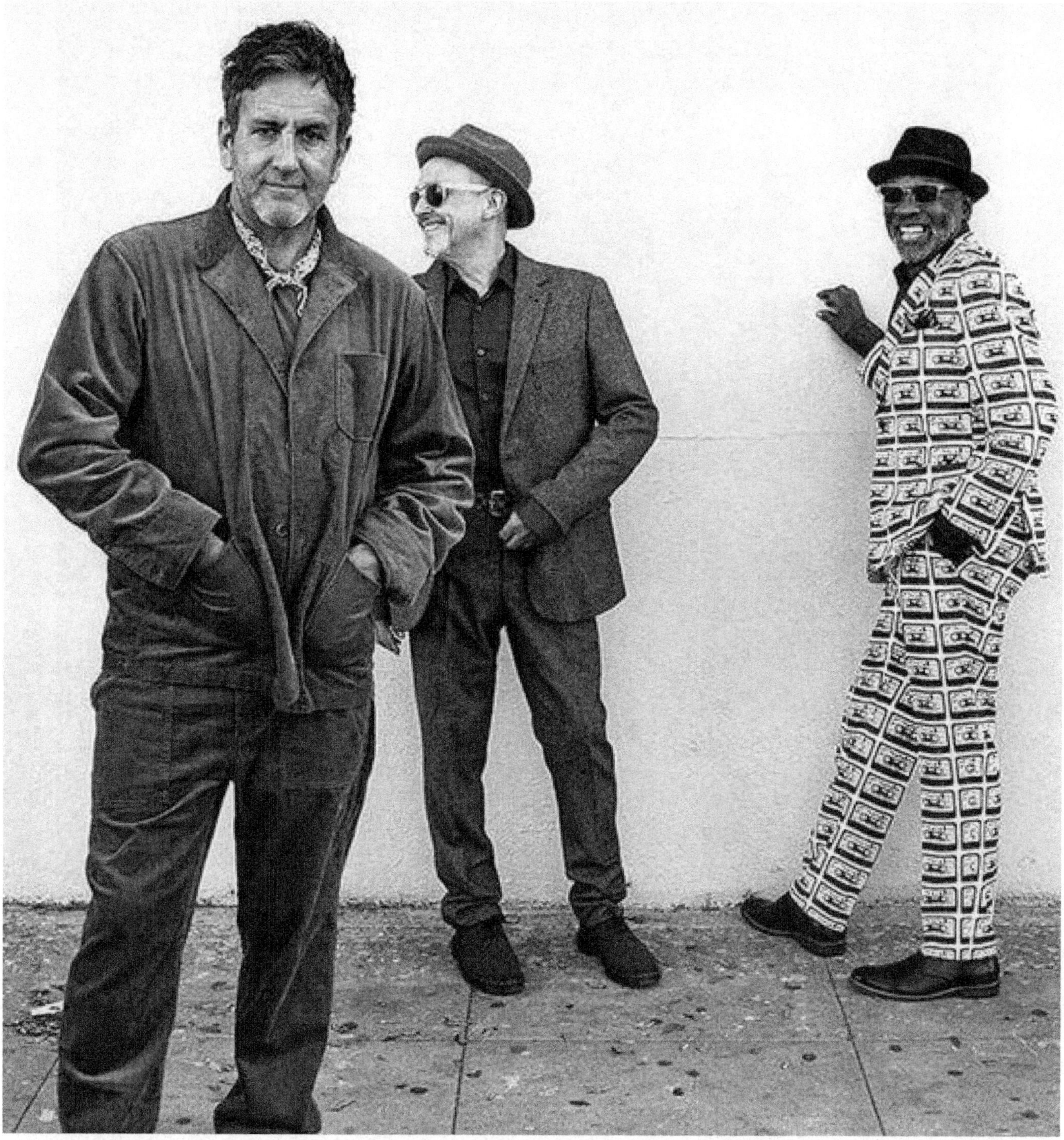

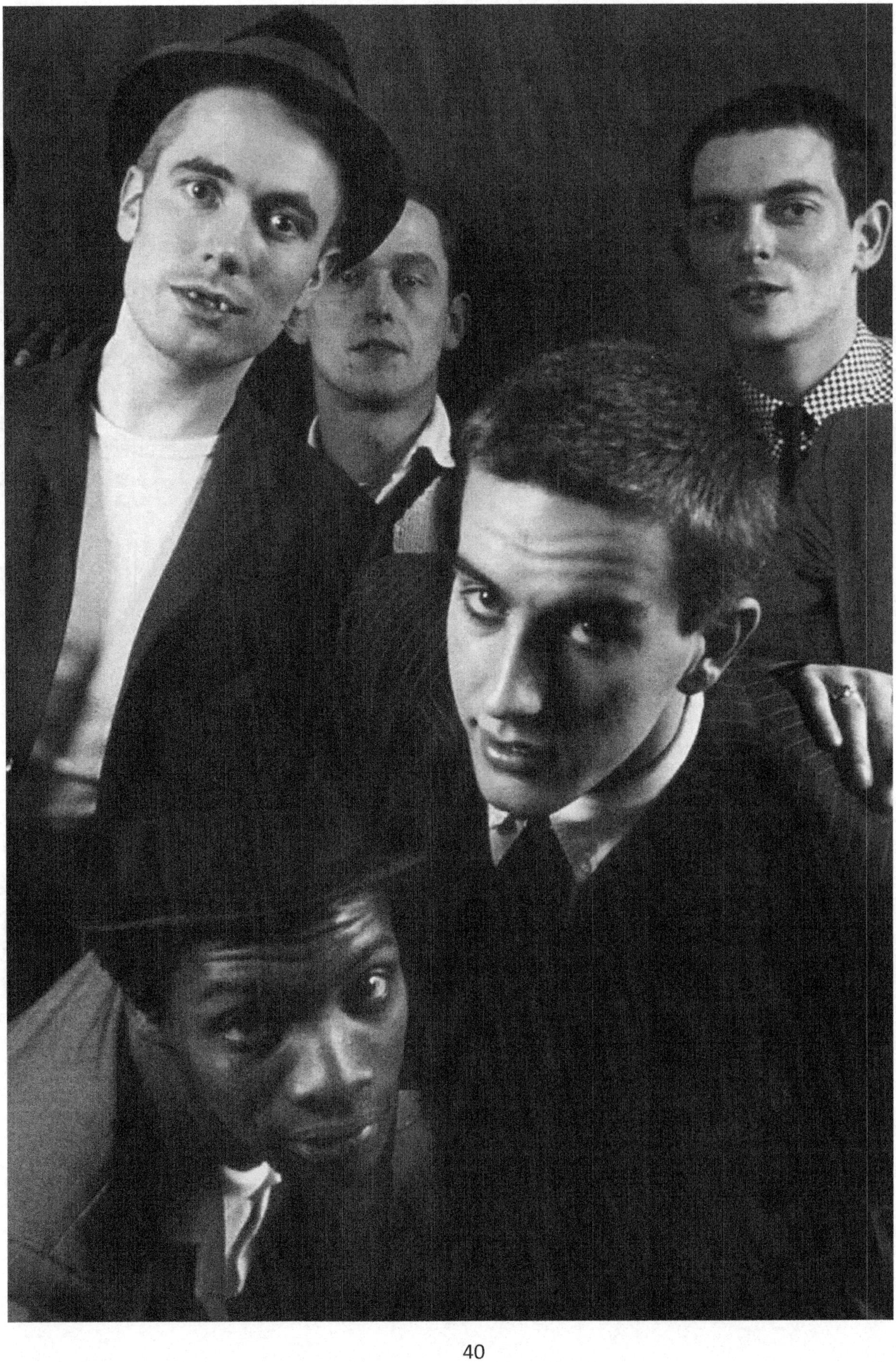

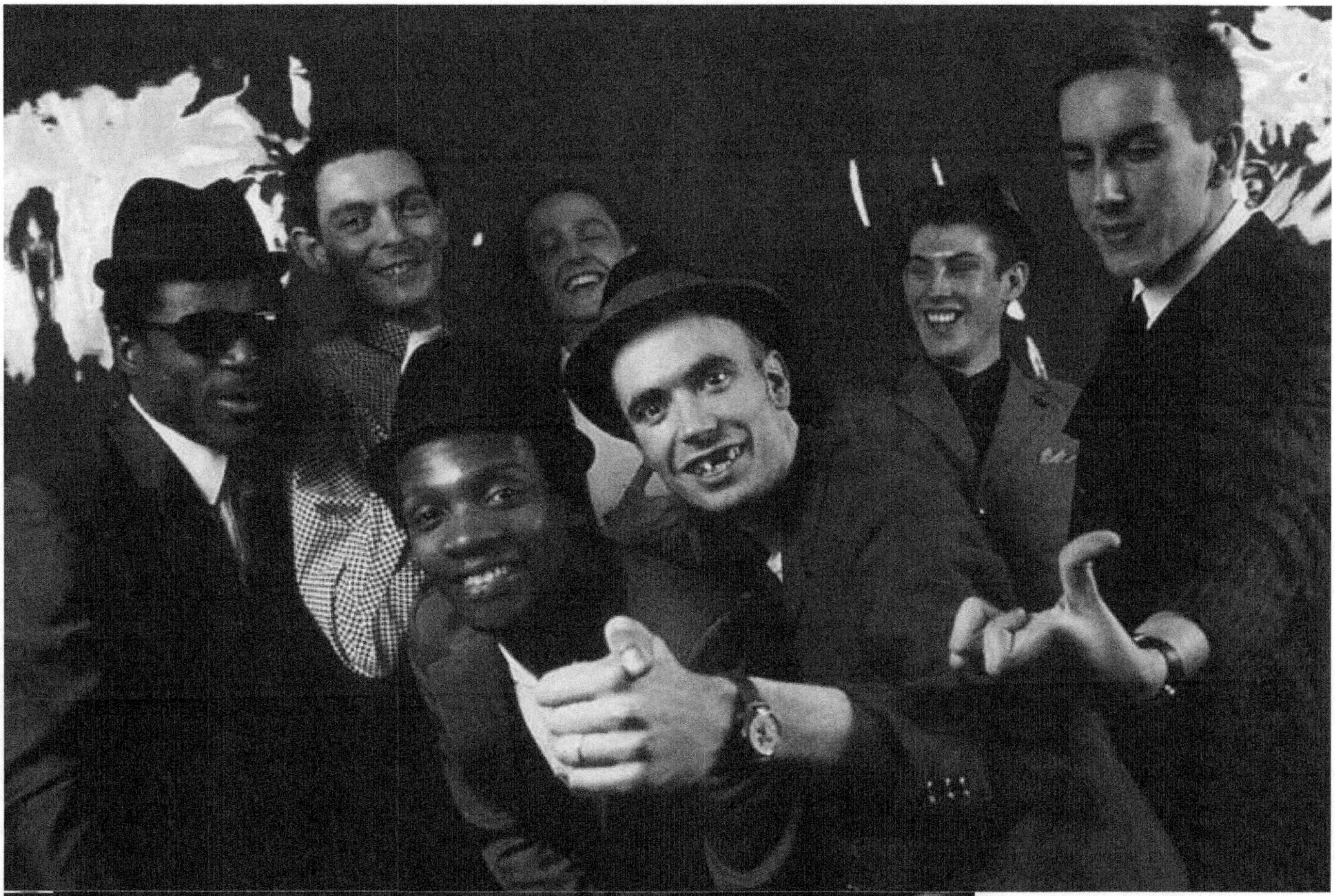

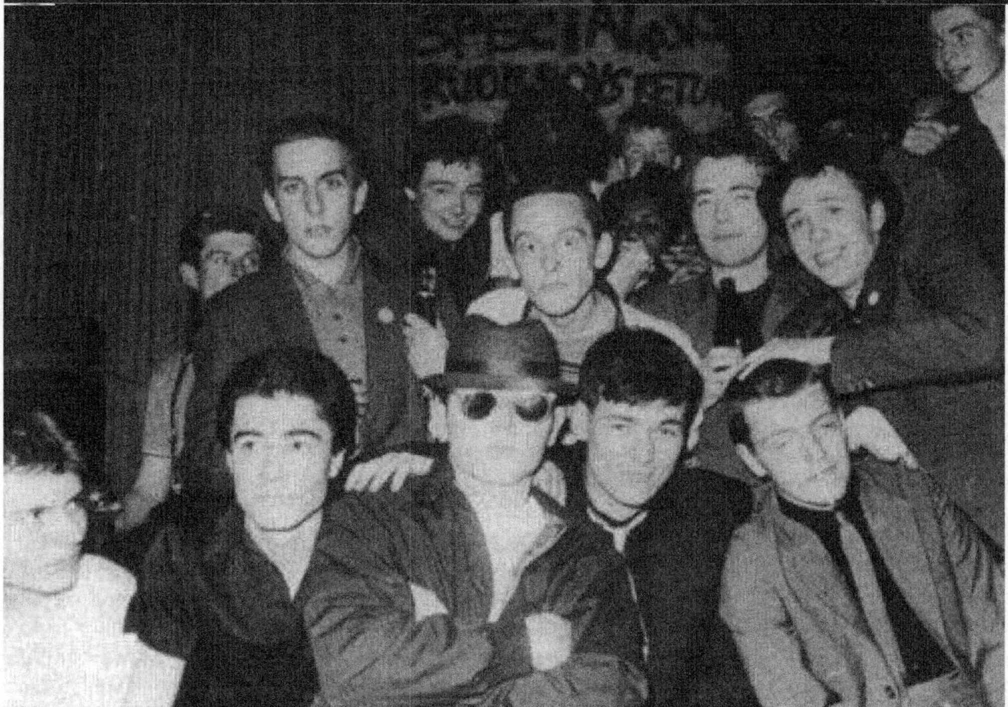

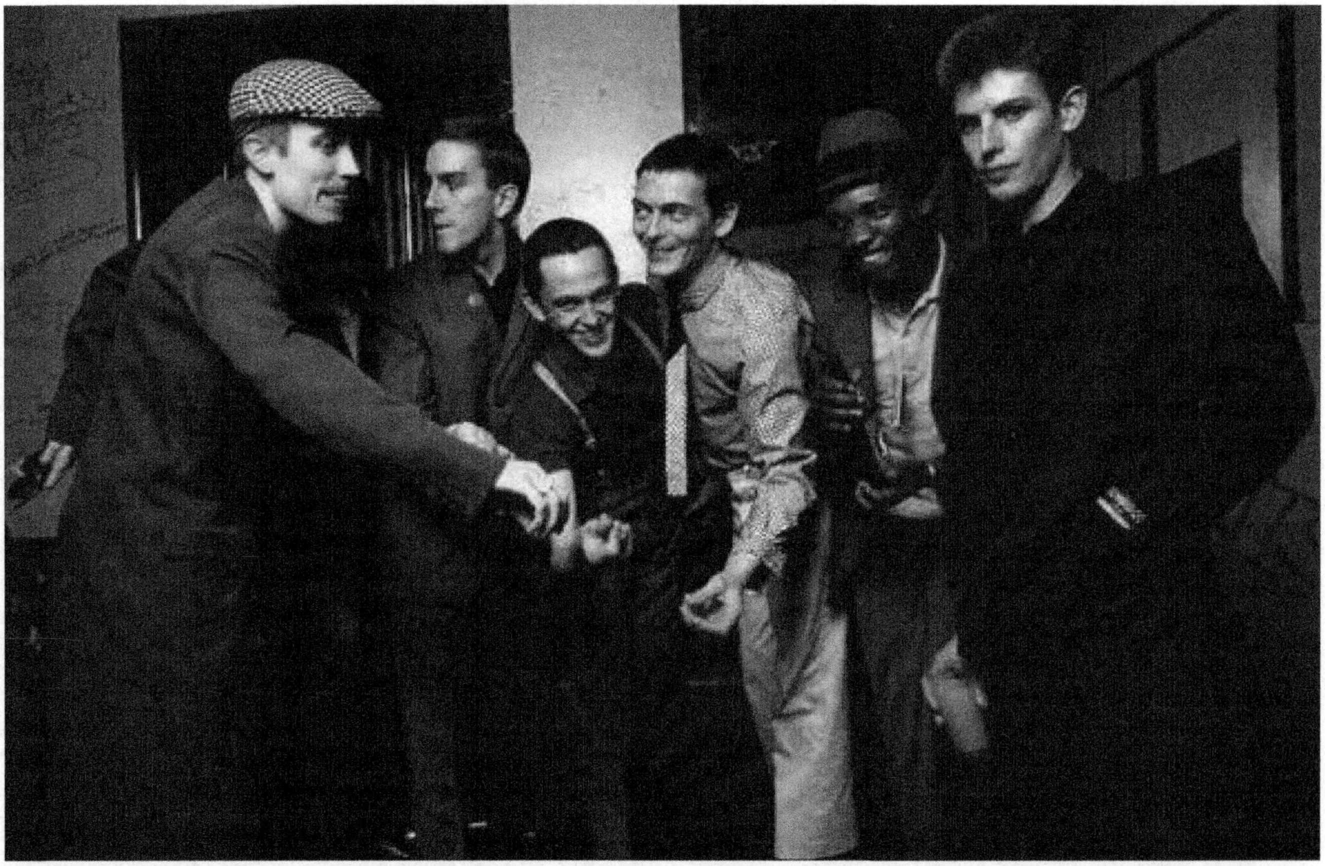

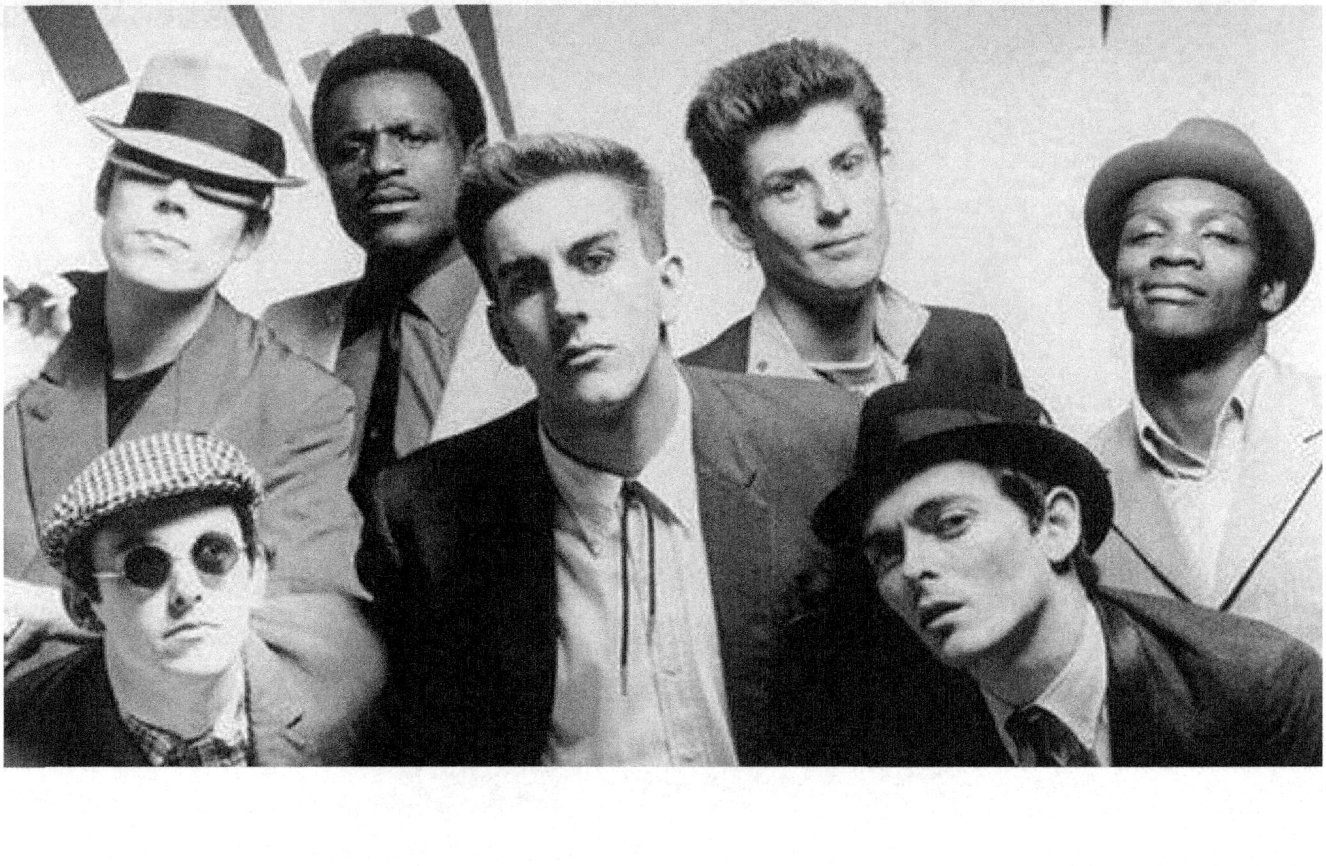

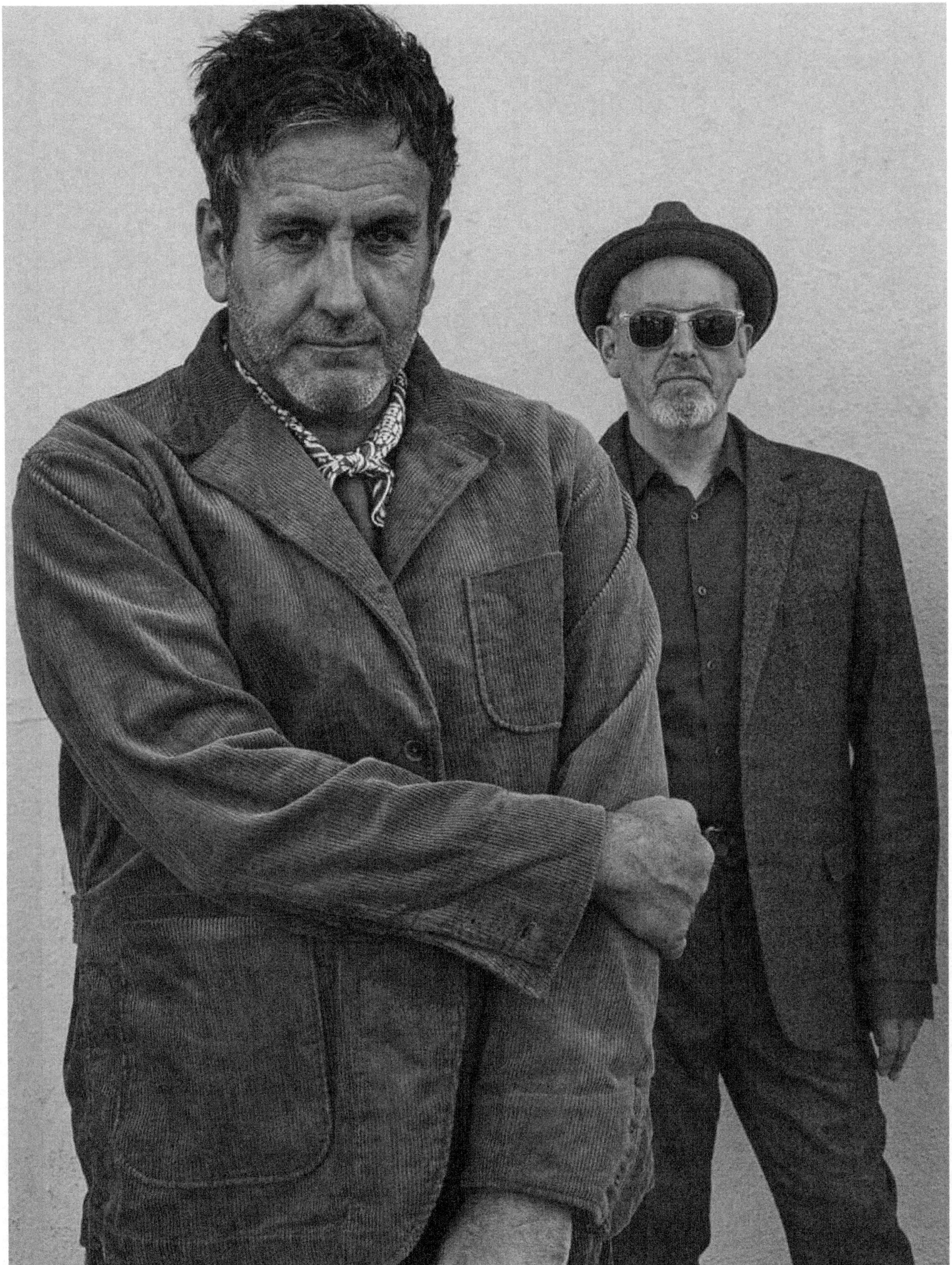

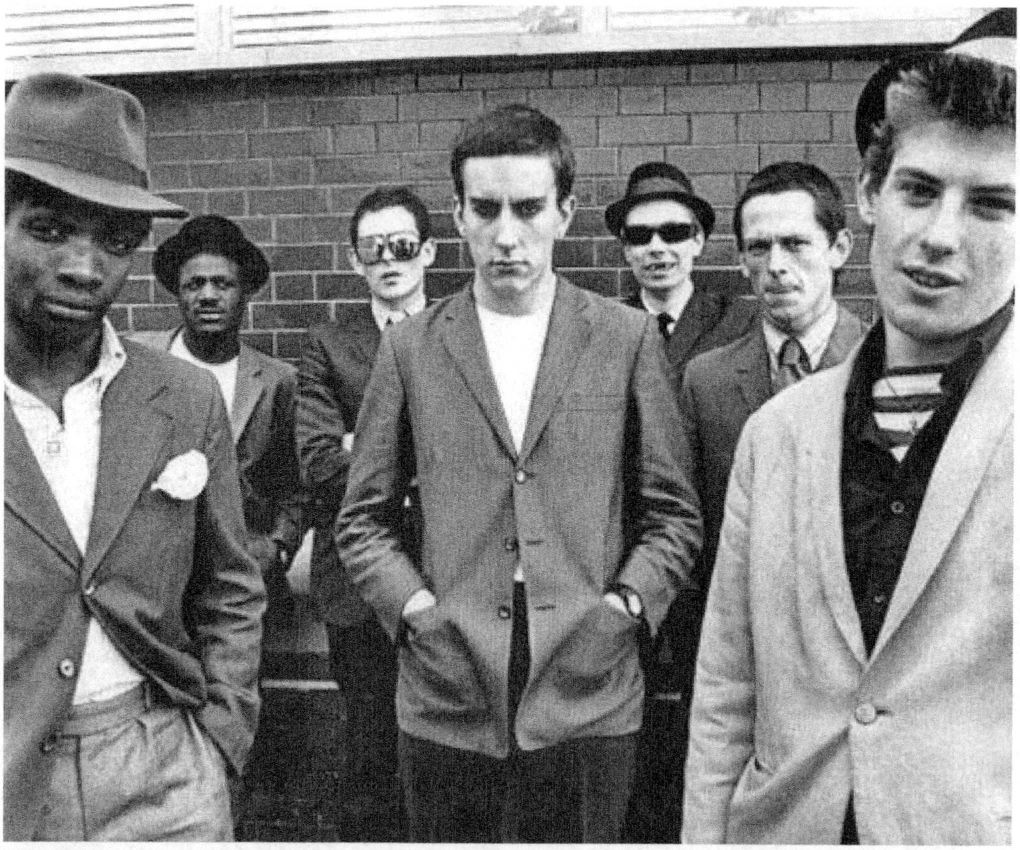

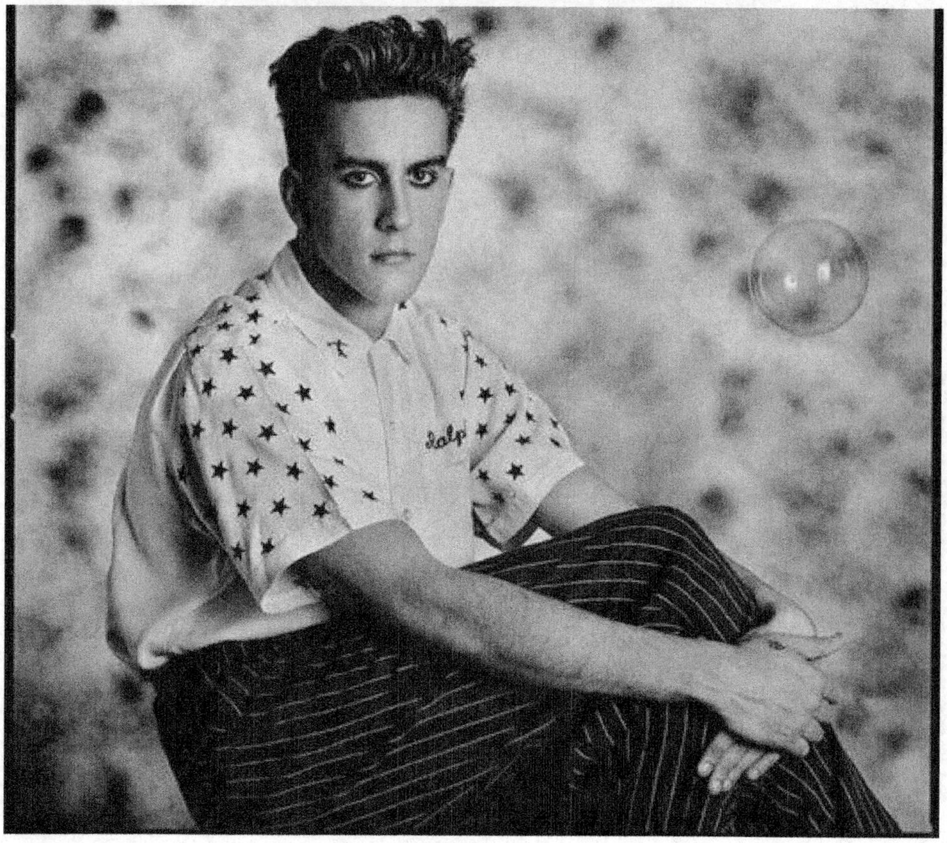

45

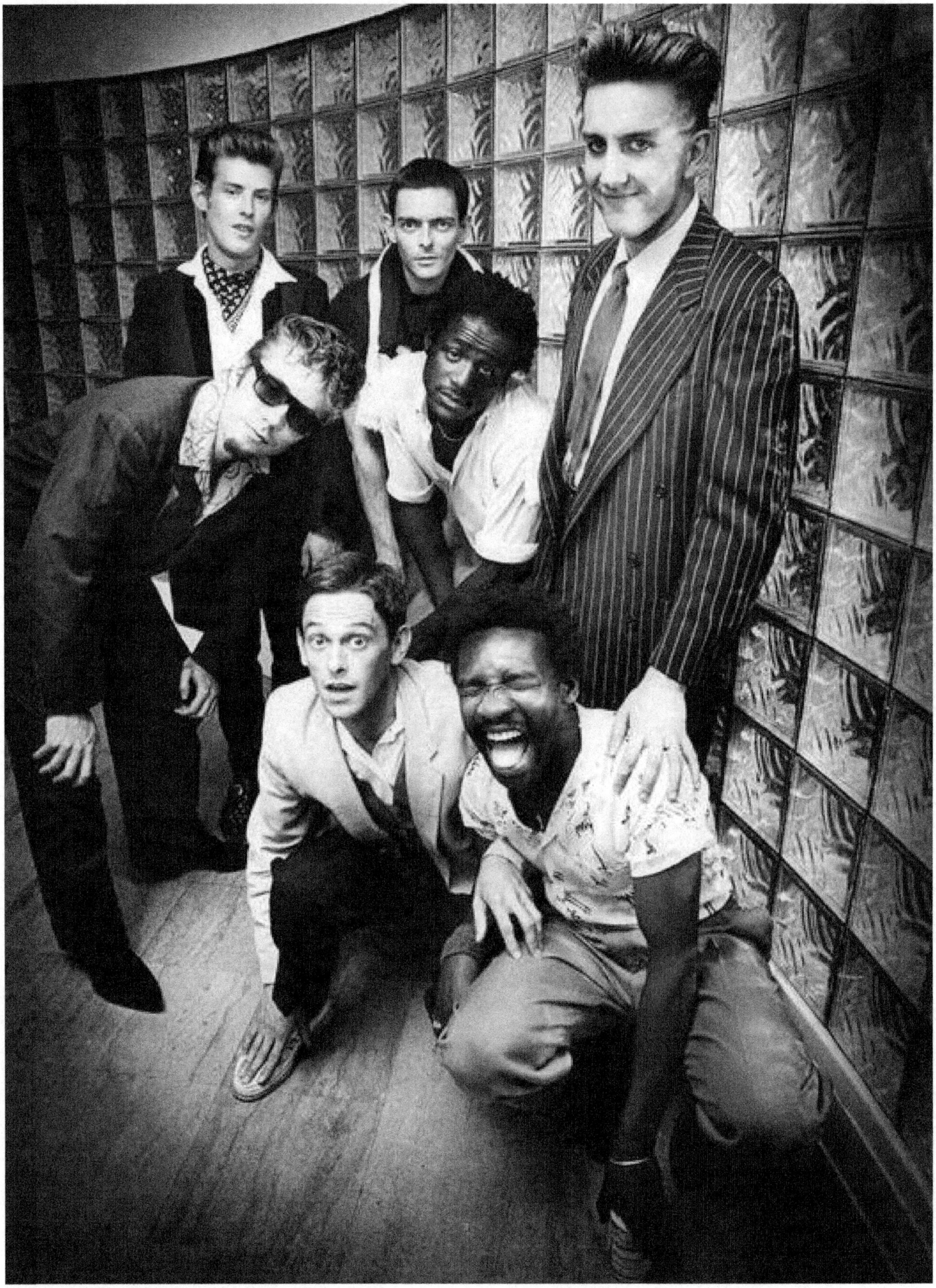

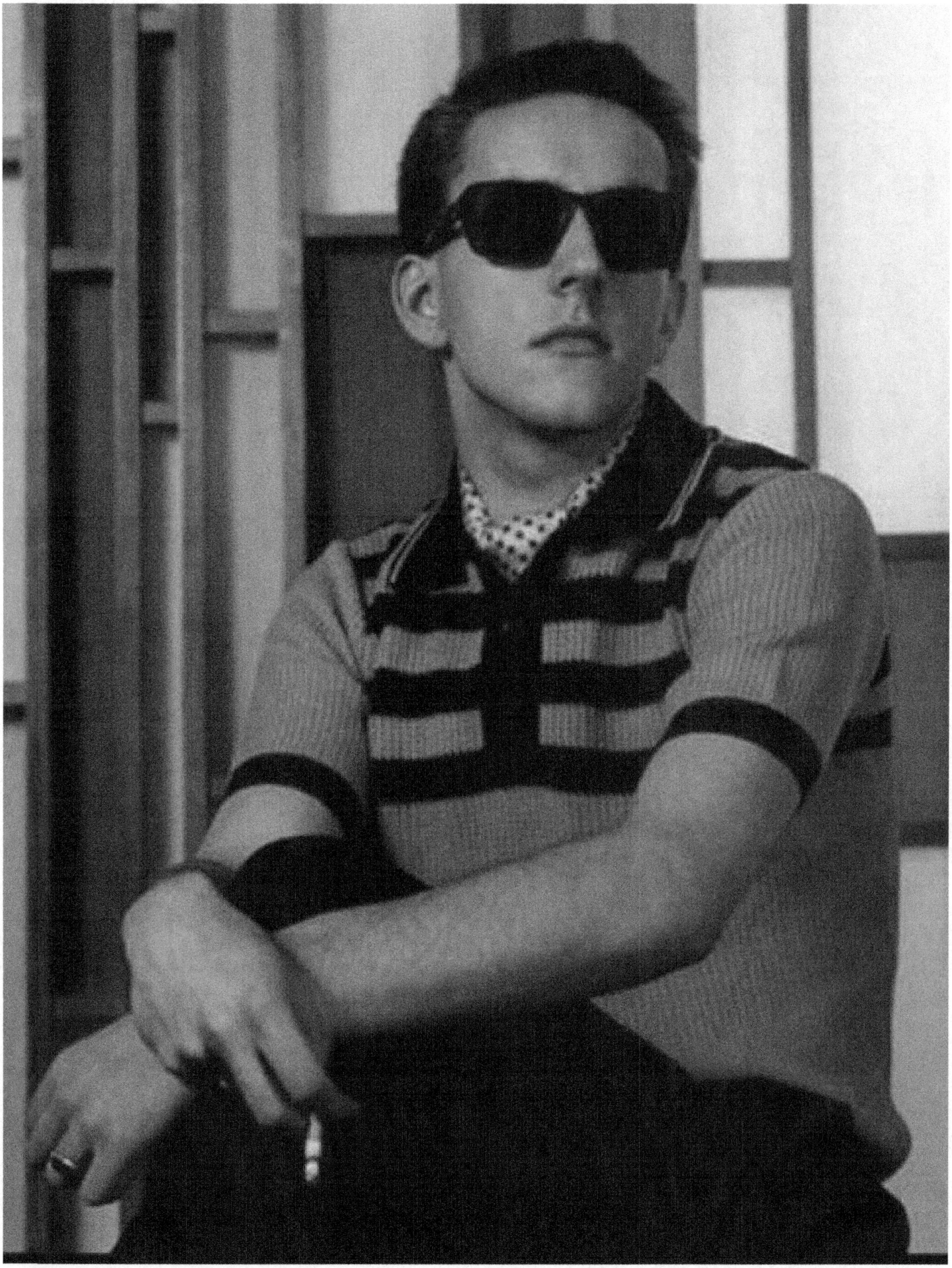

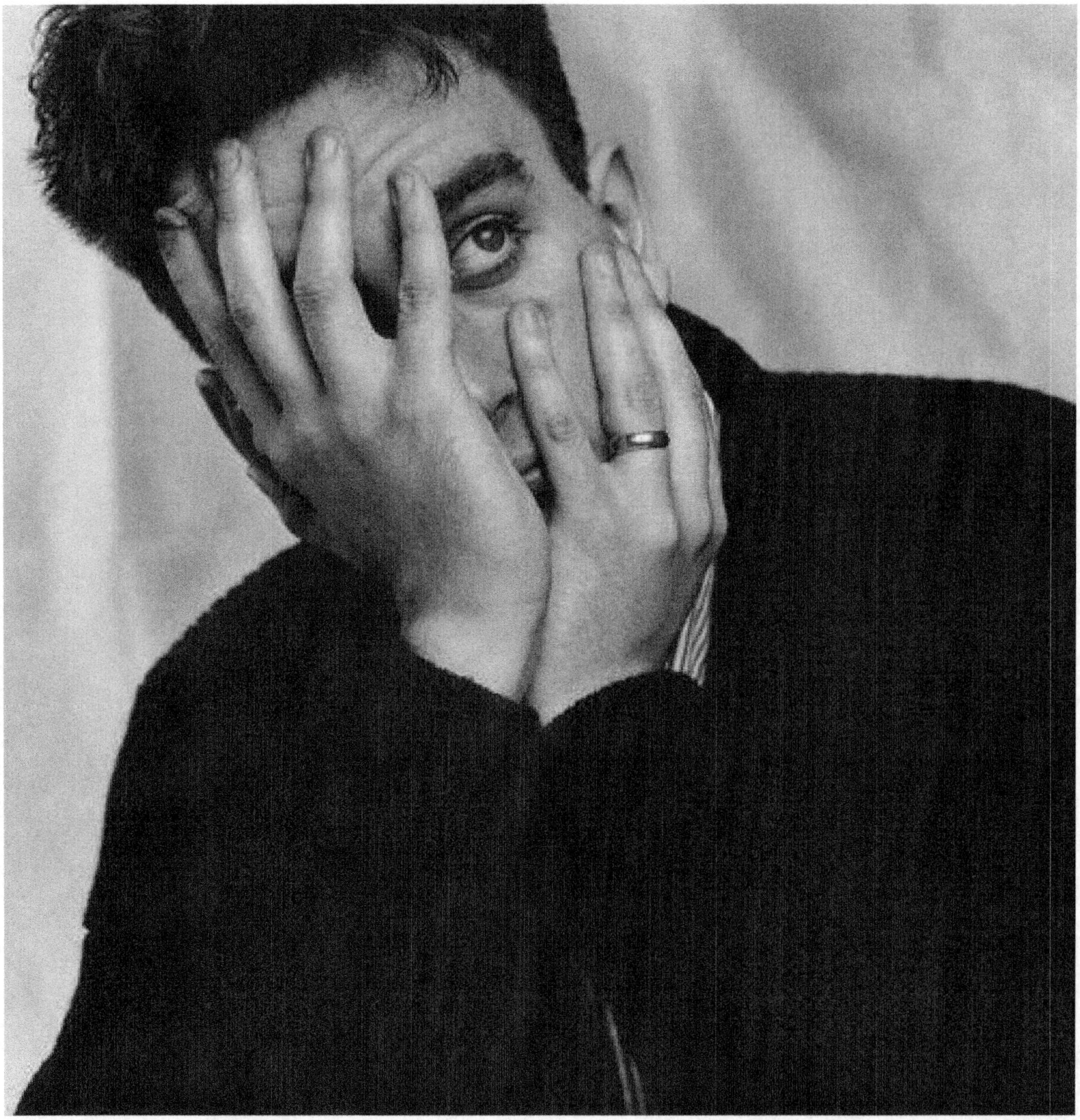

THE SPECIALS

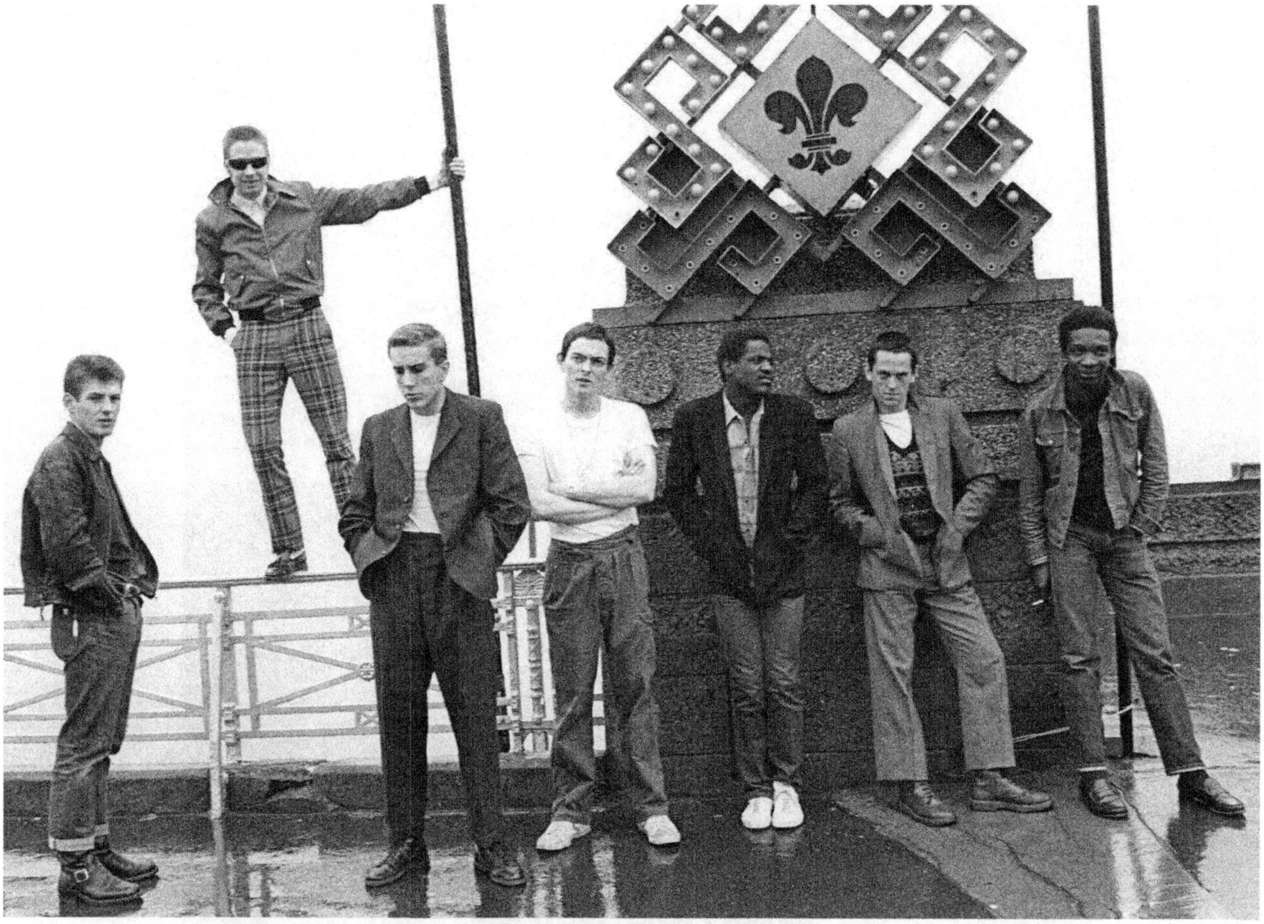

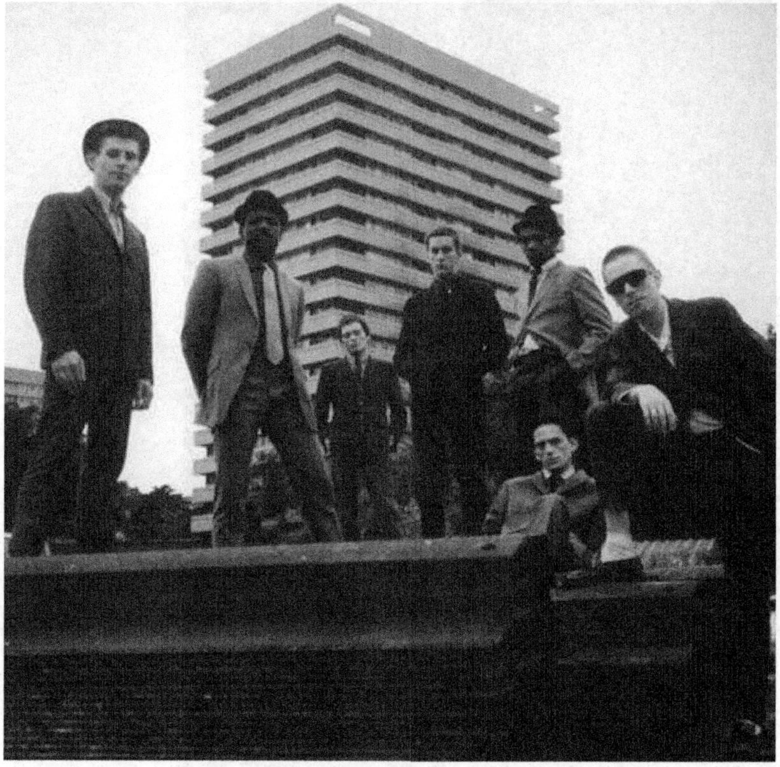

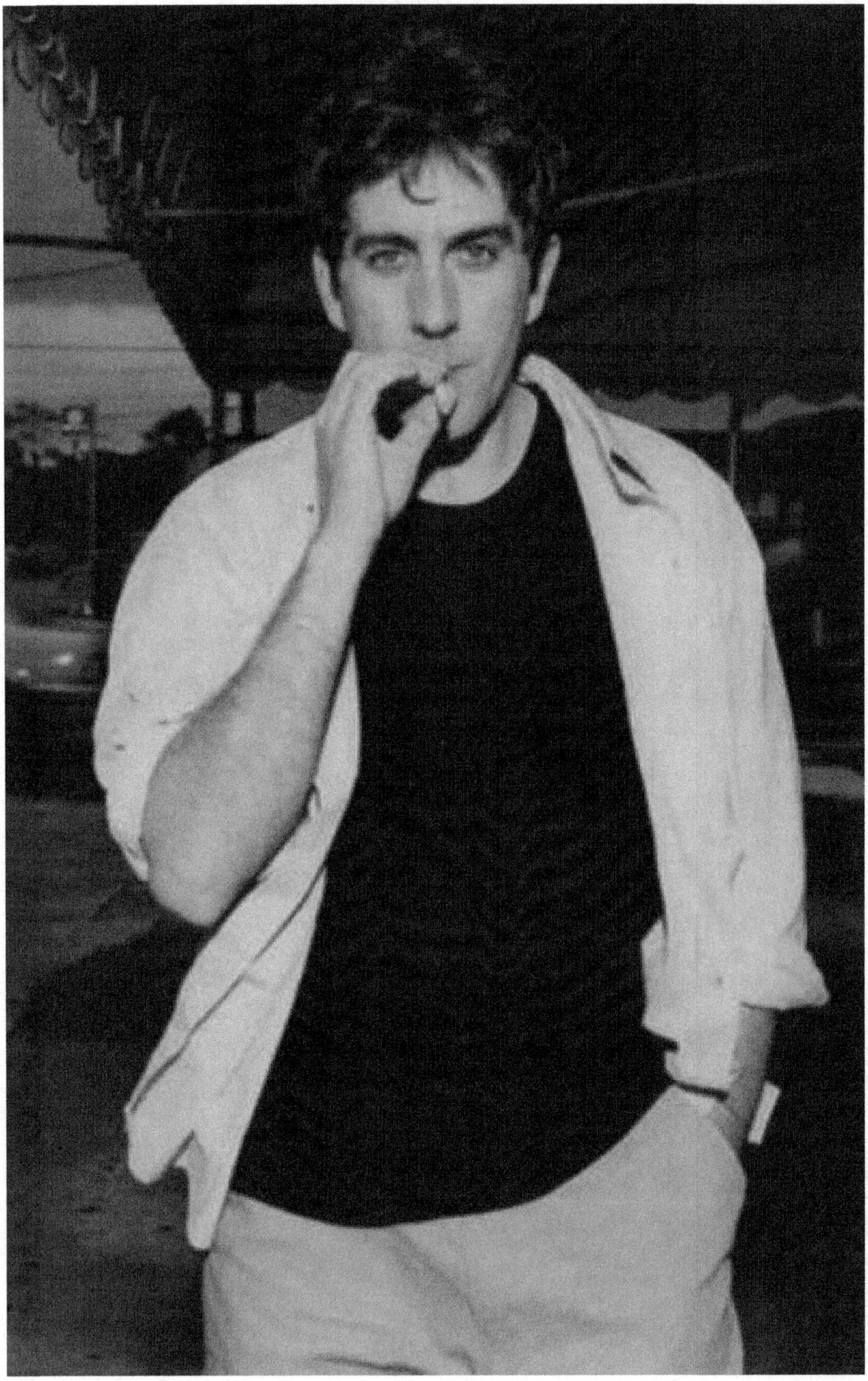

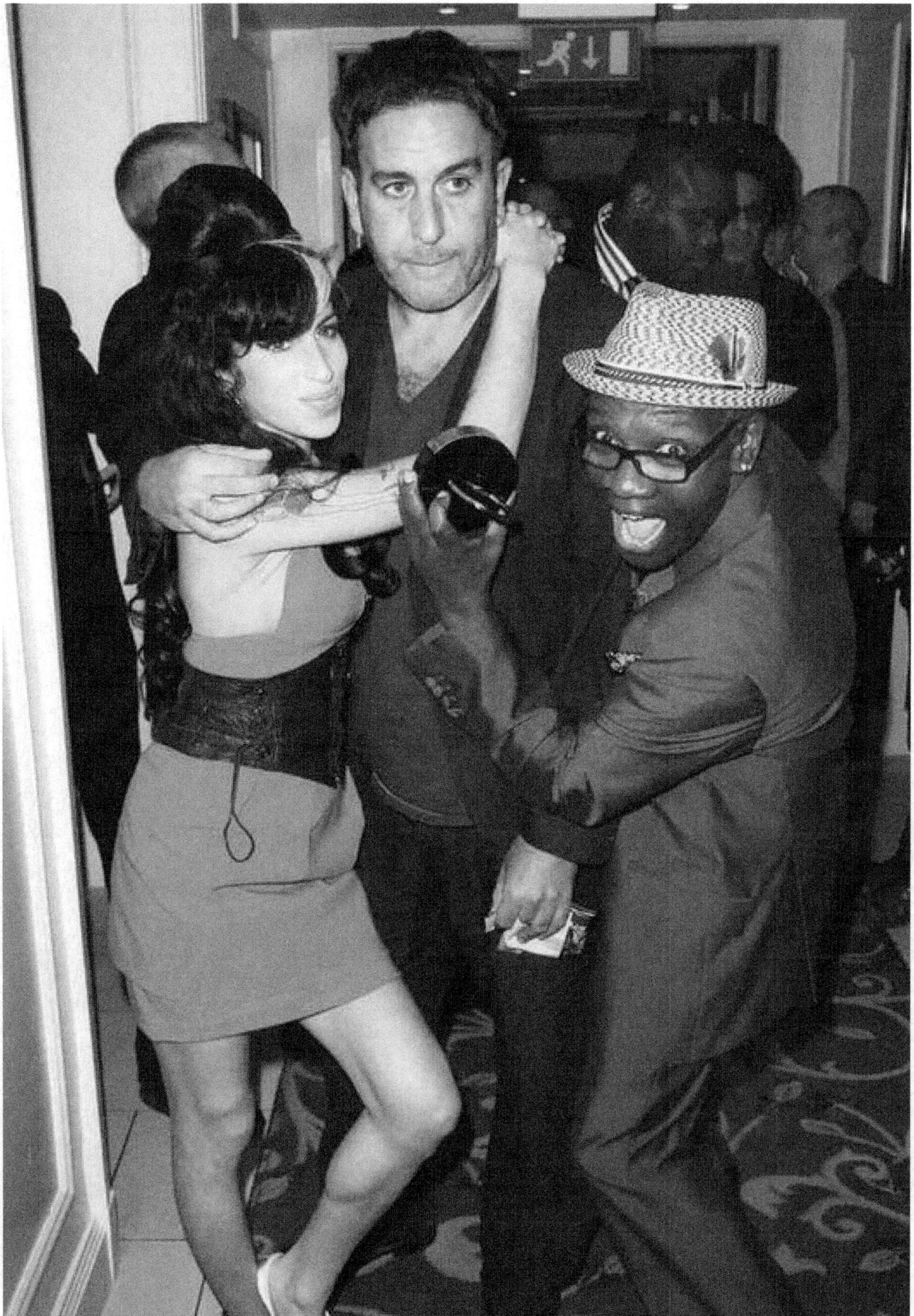

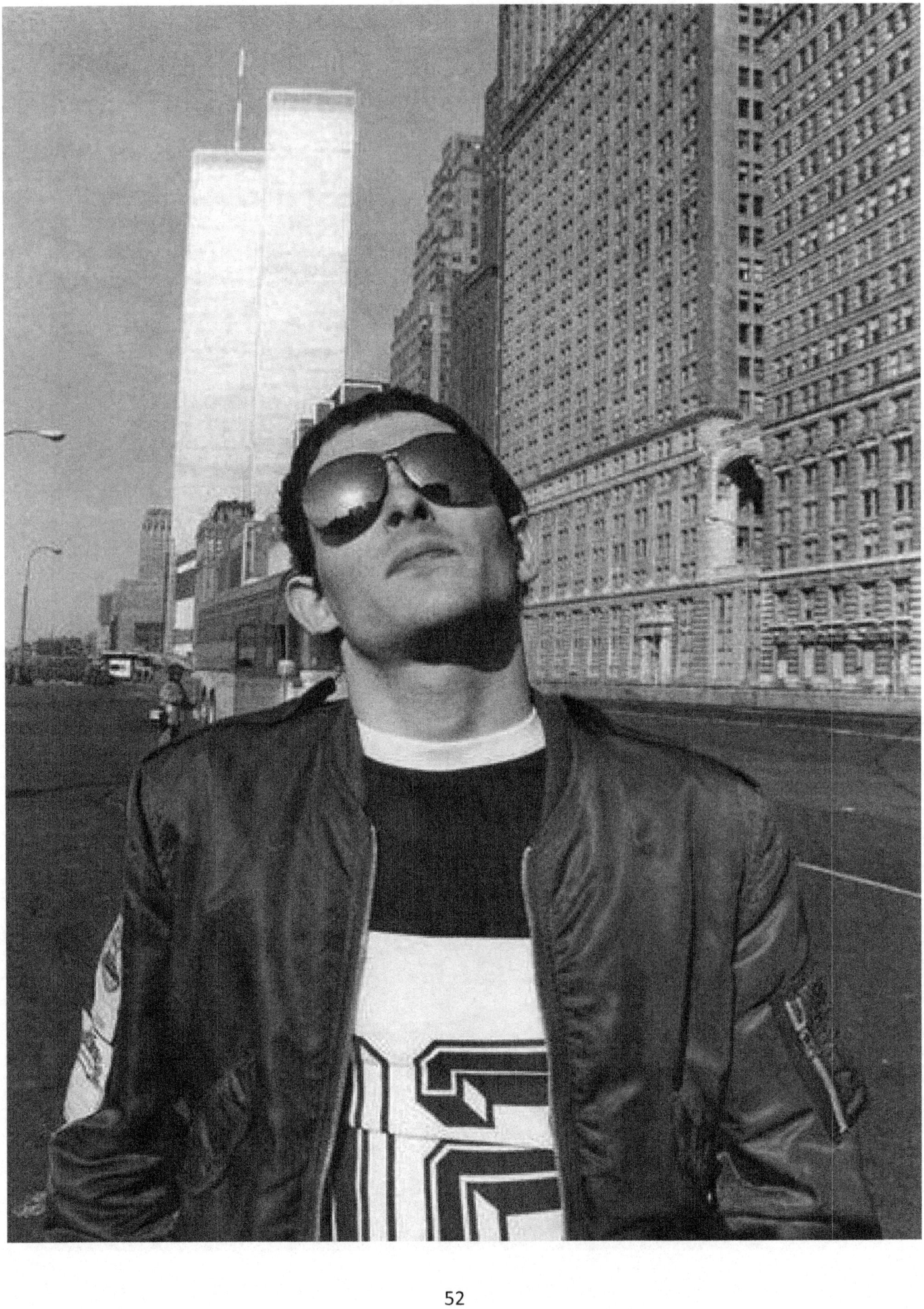

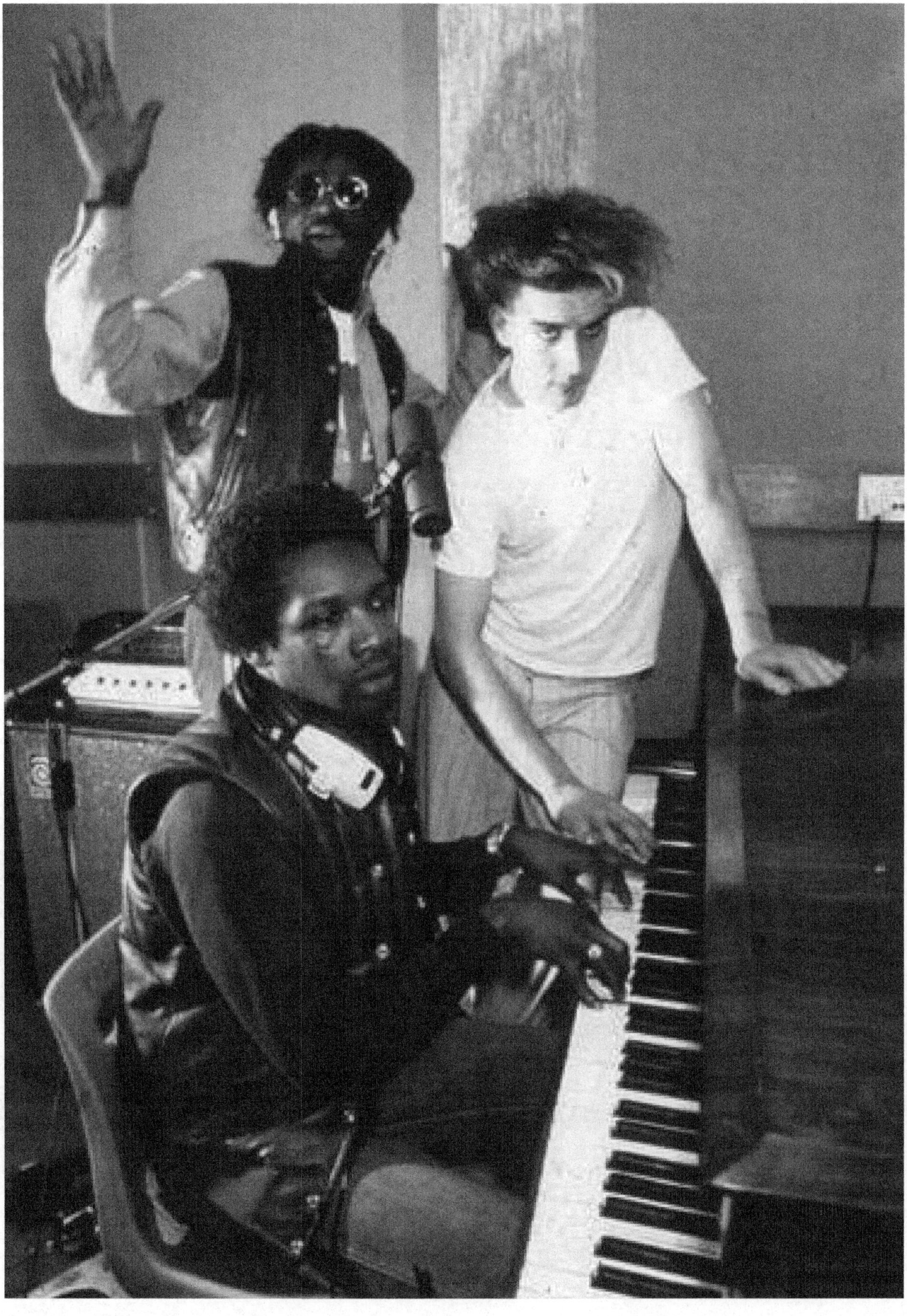

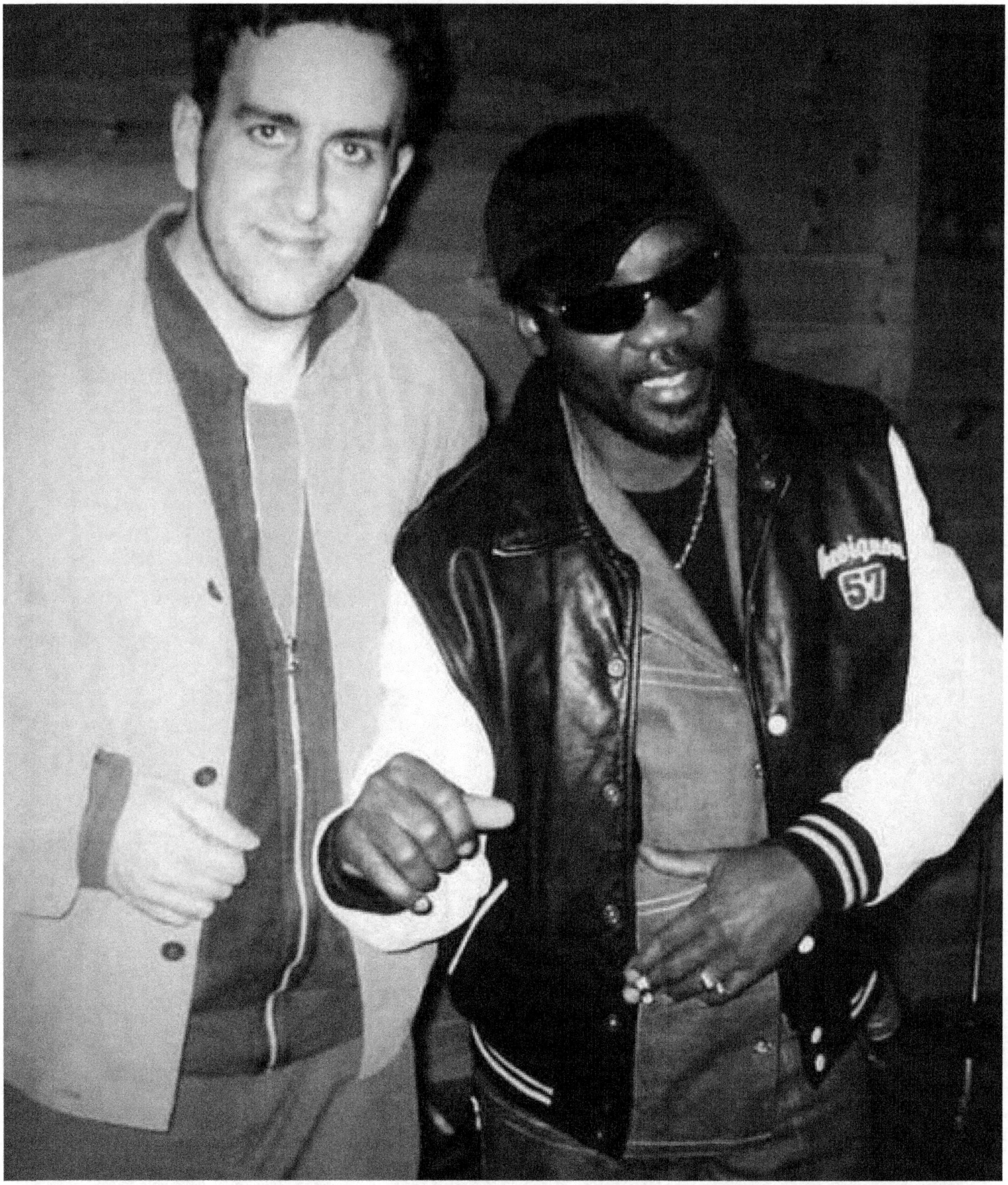
57

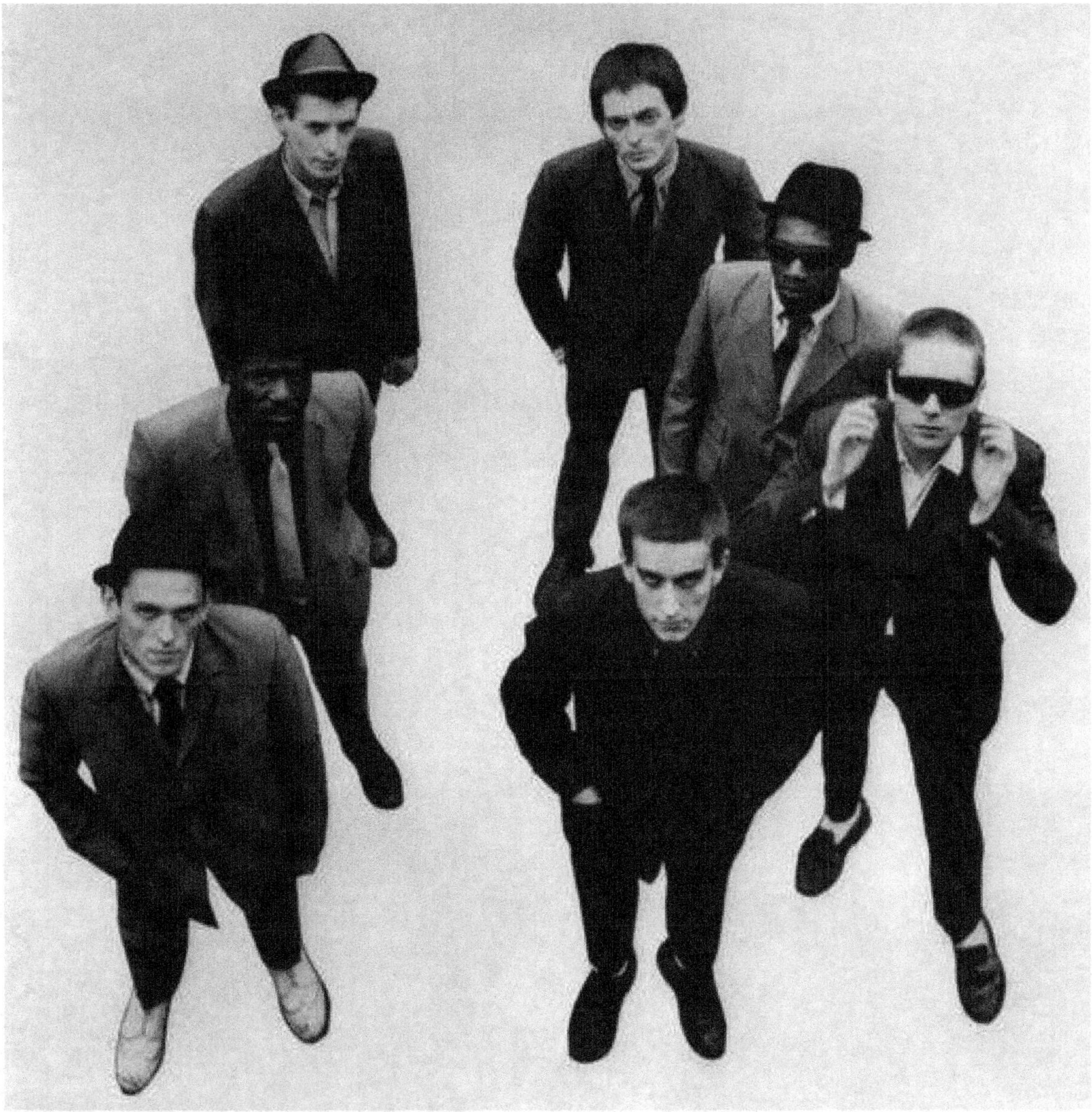

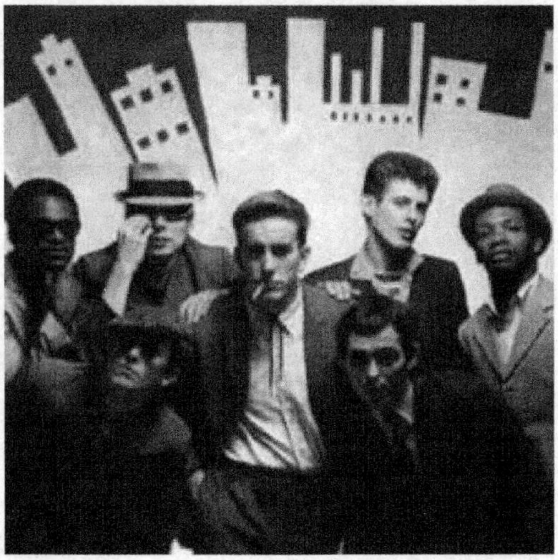

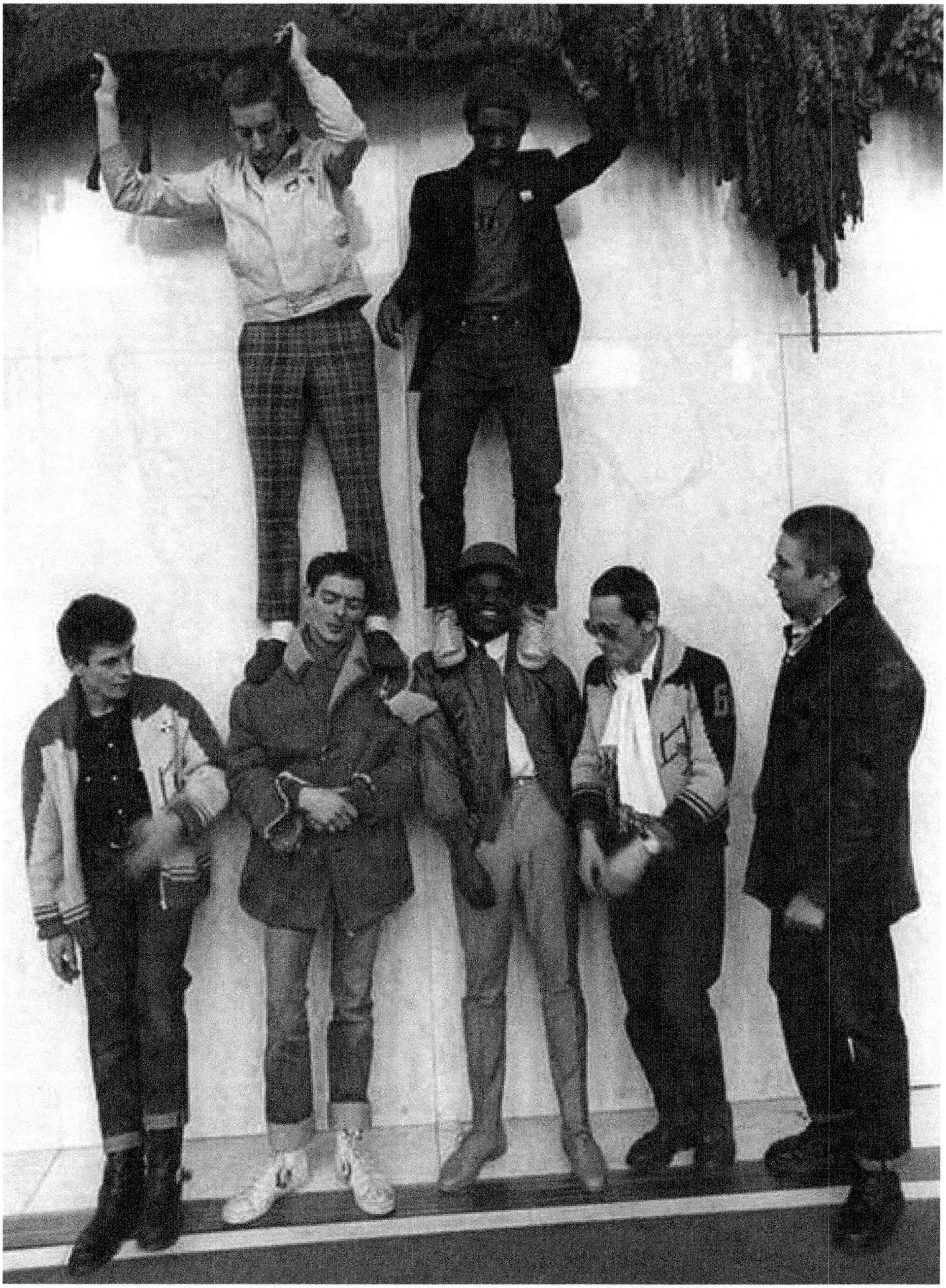

57

58

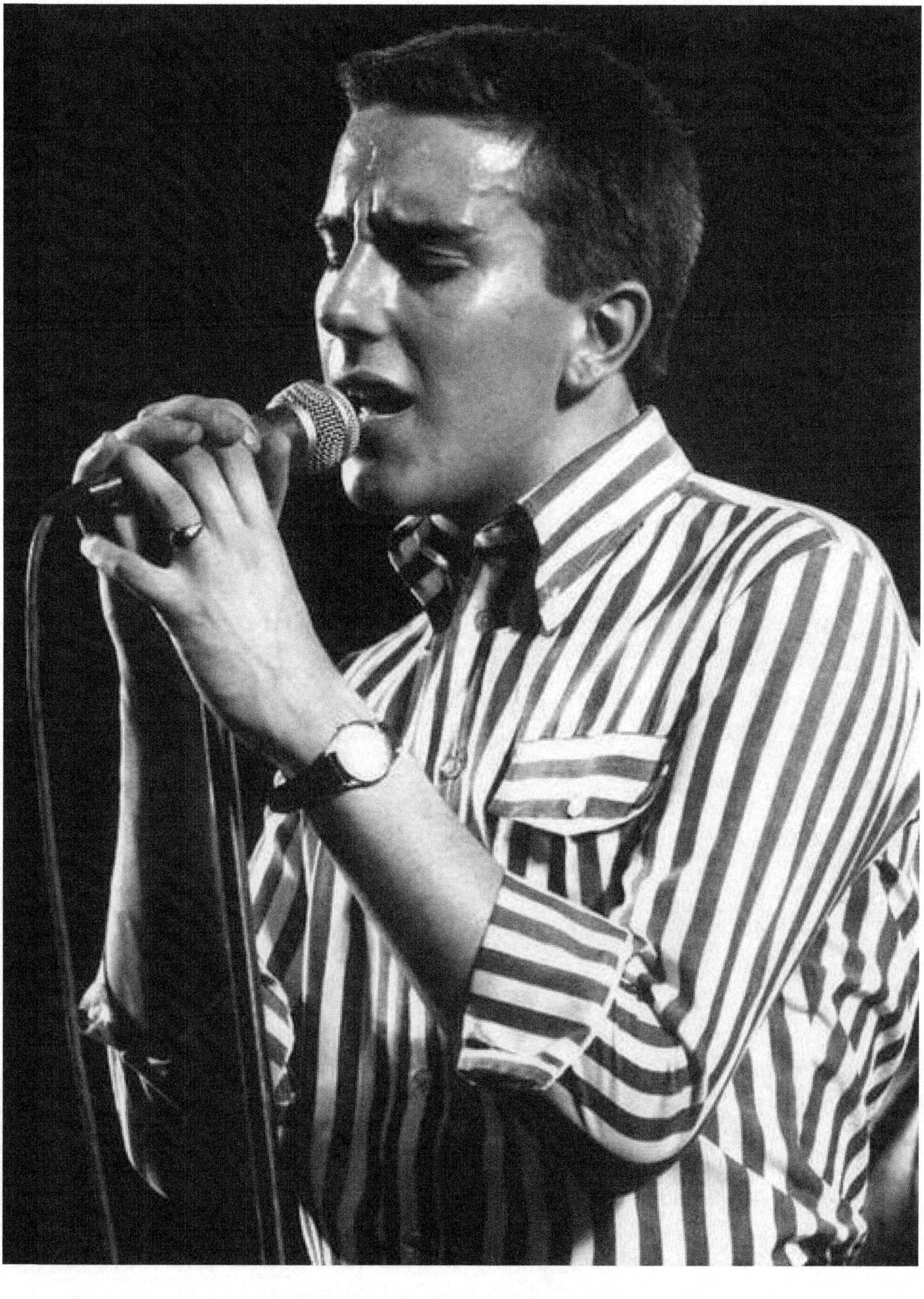

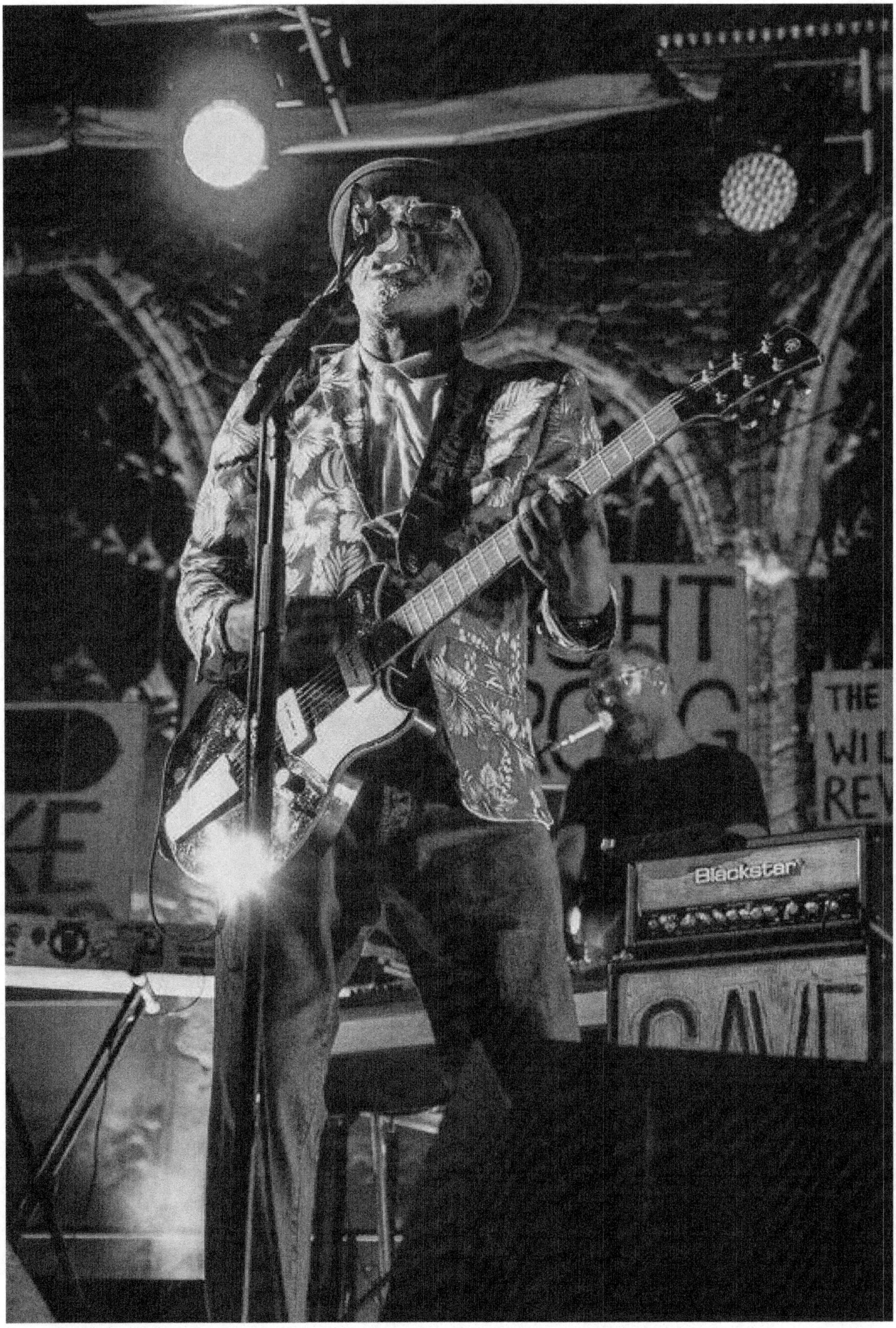
THE
Blackstar

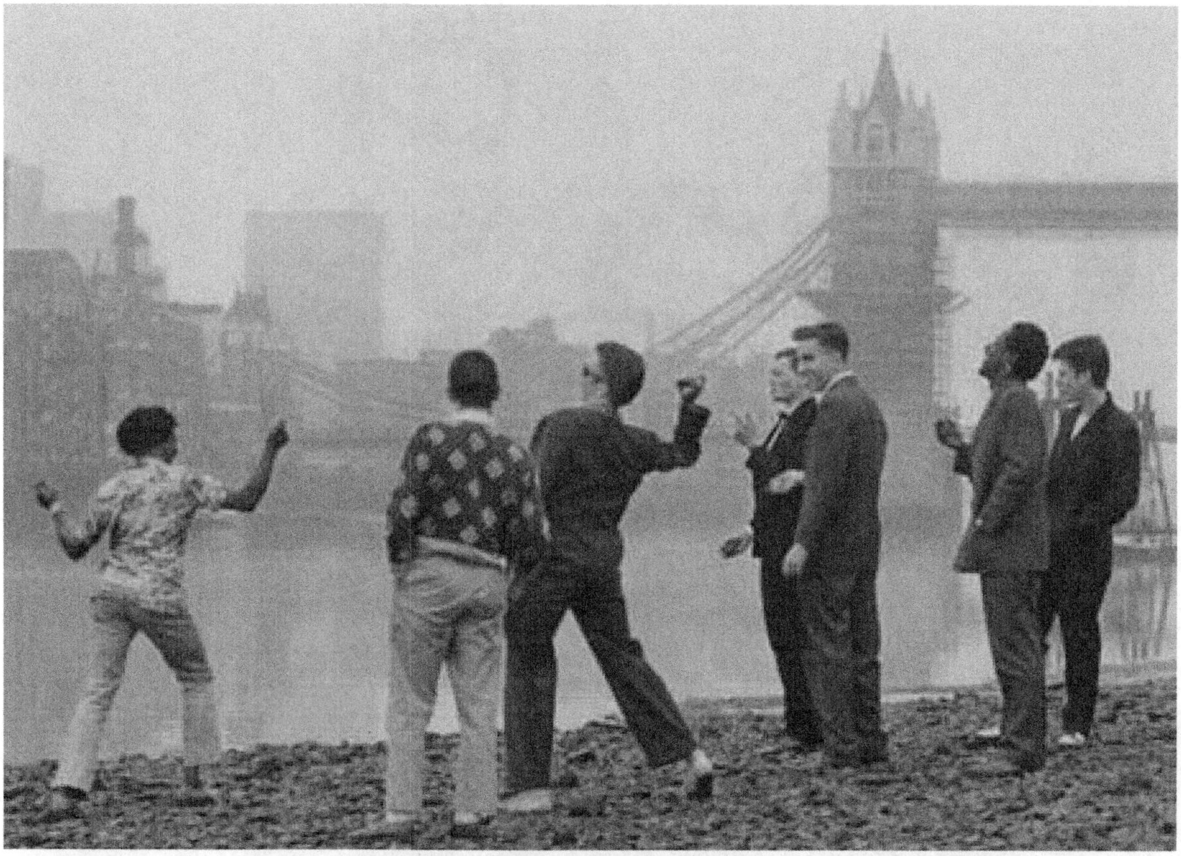

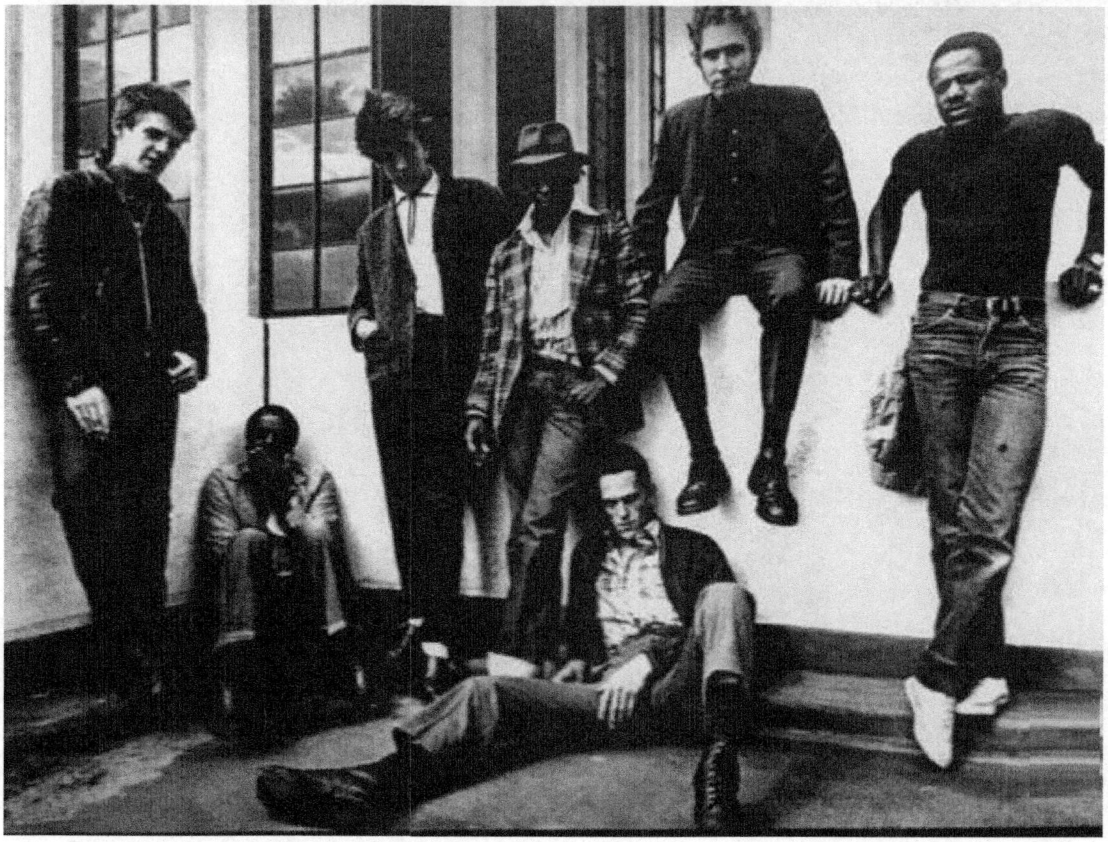

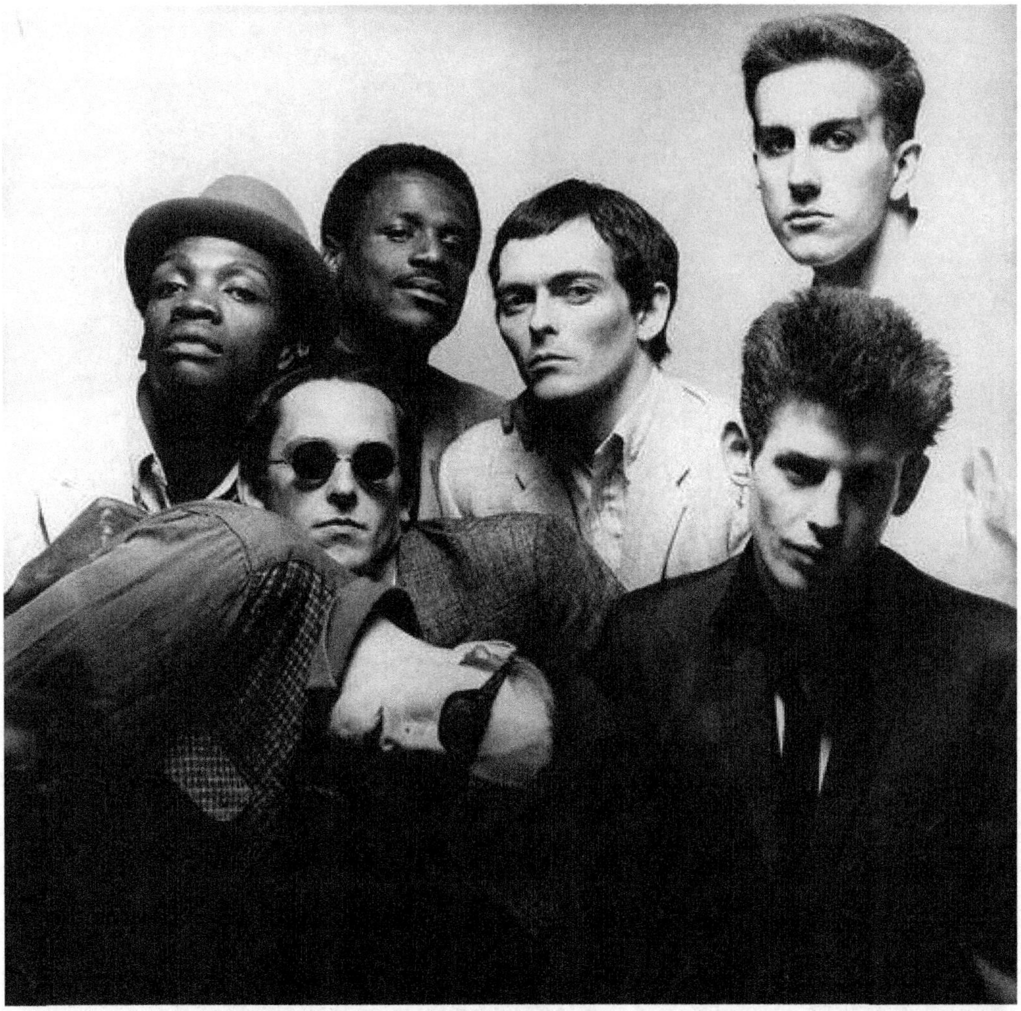

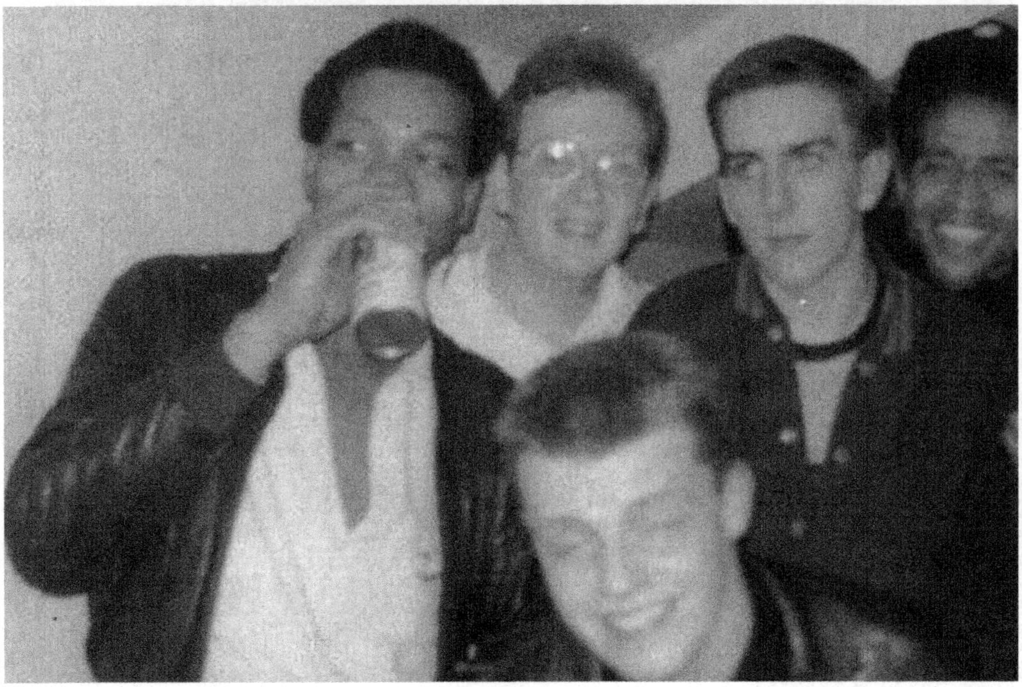

63

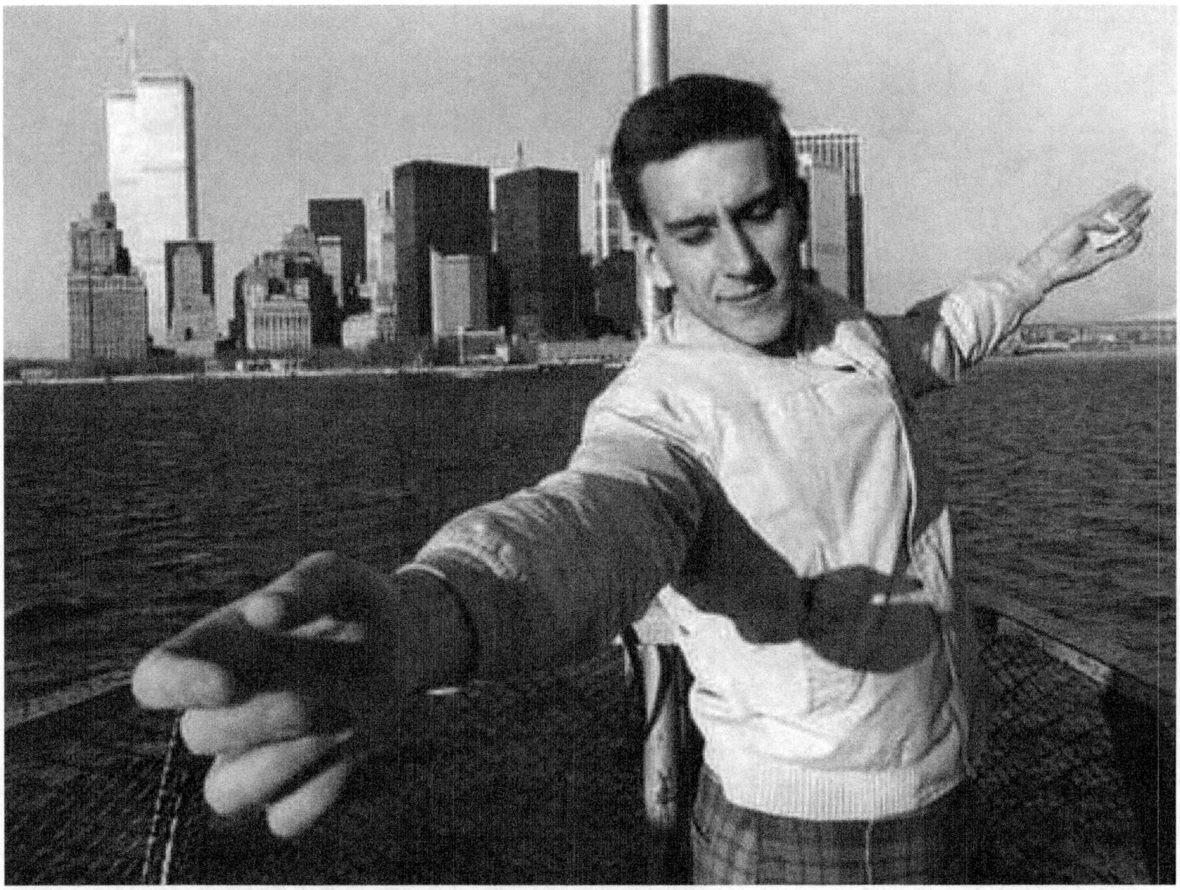

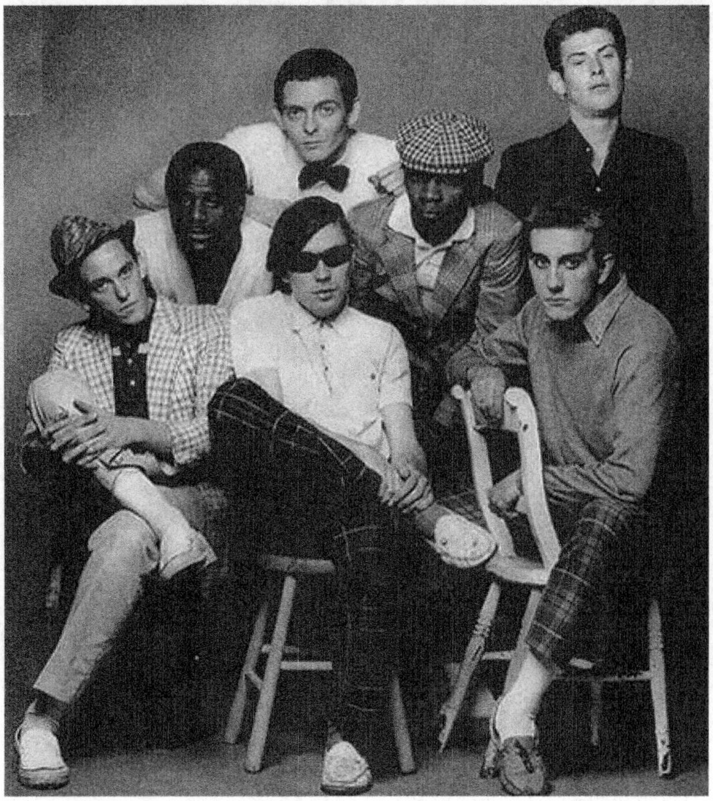

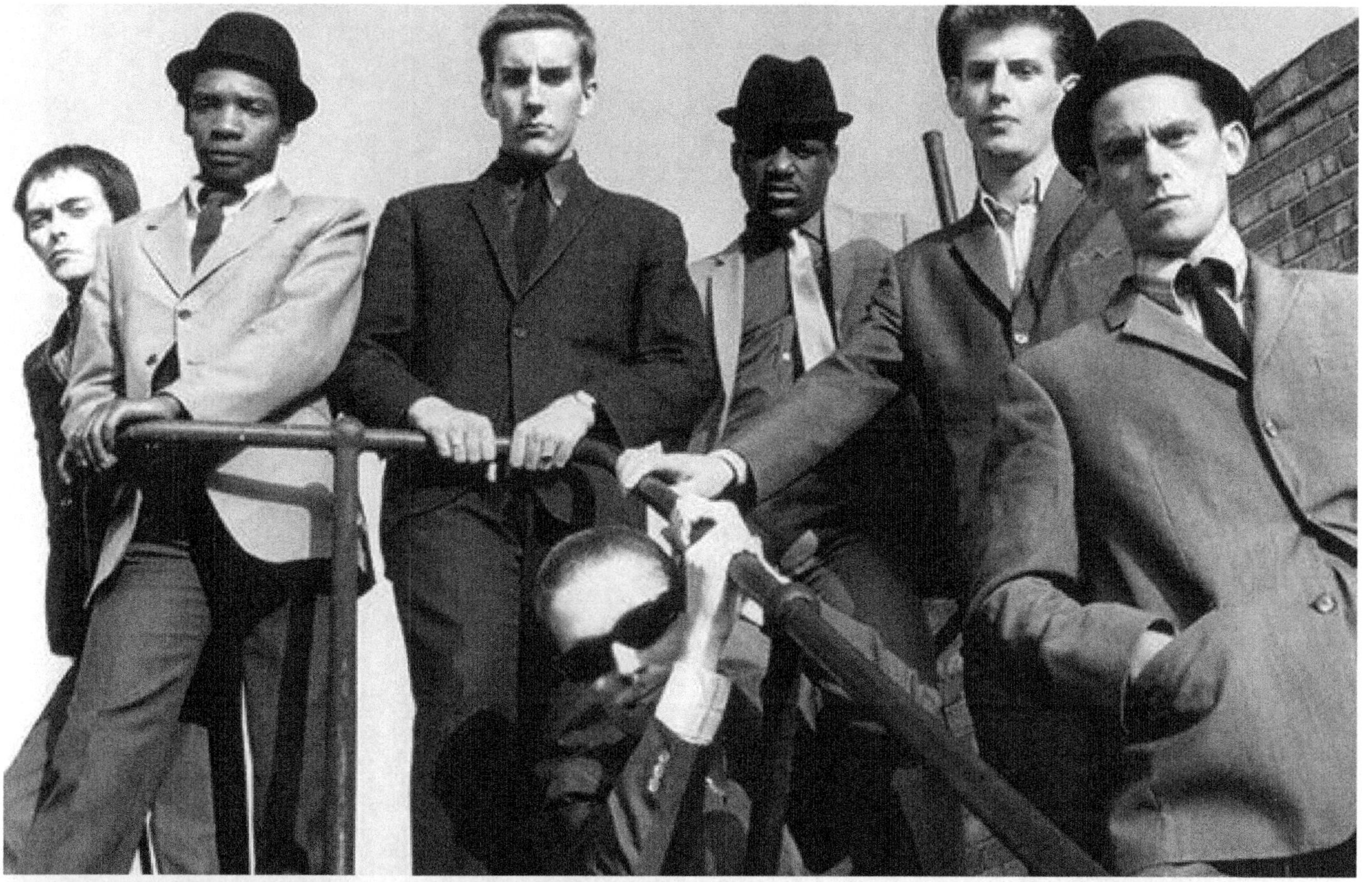

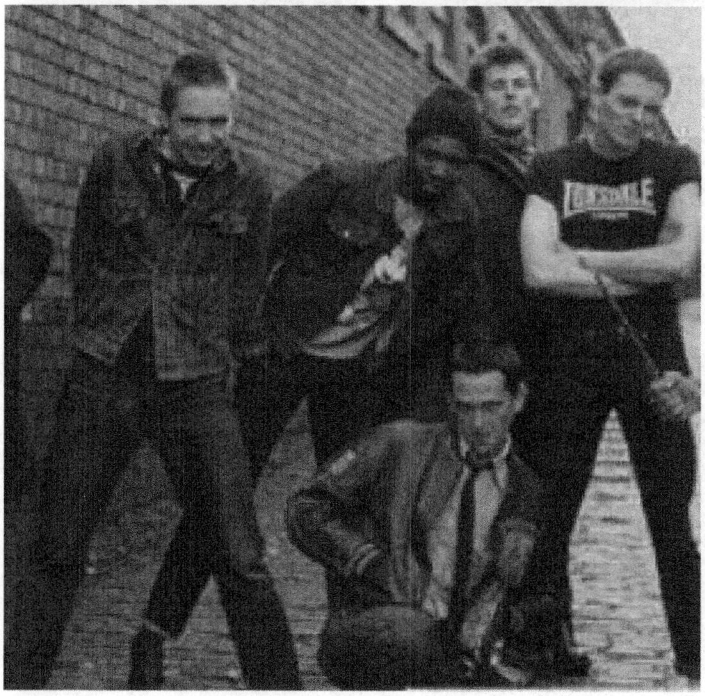

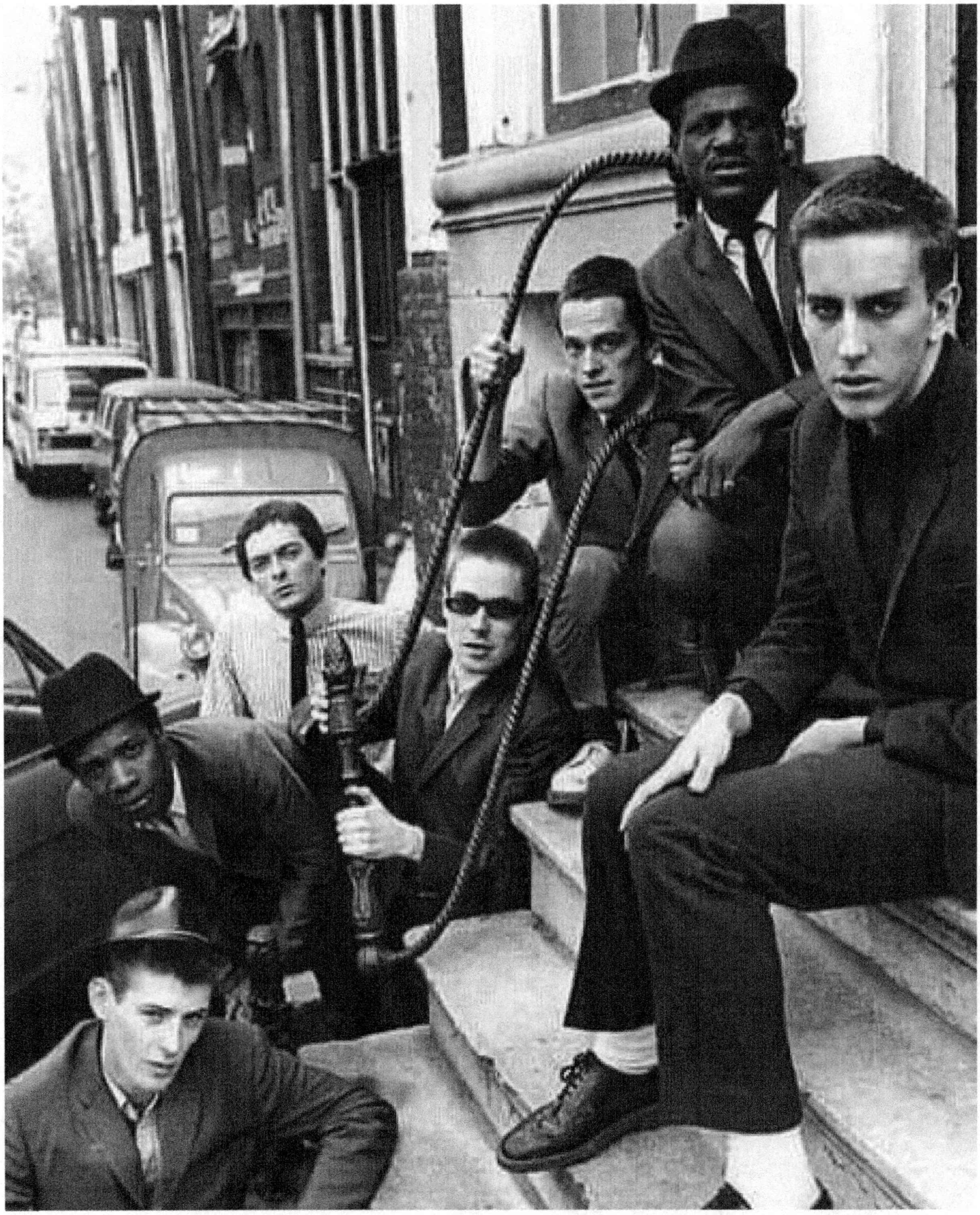

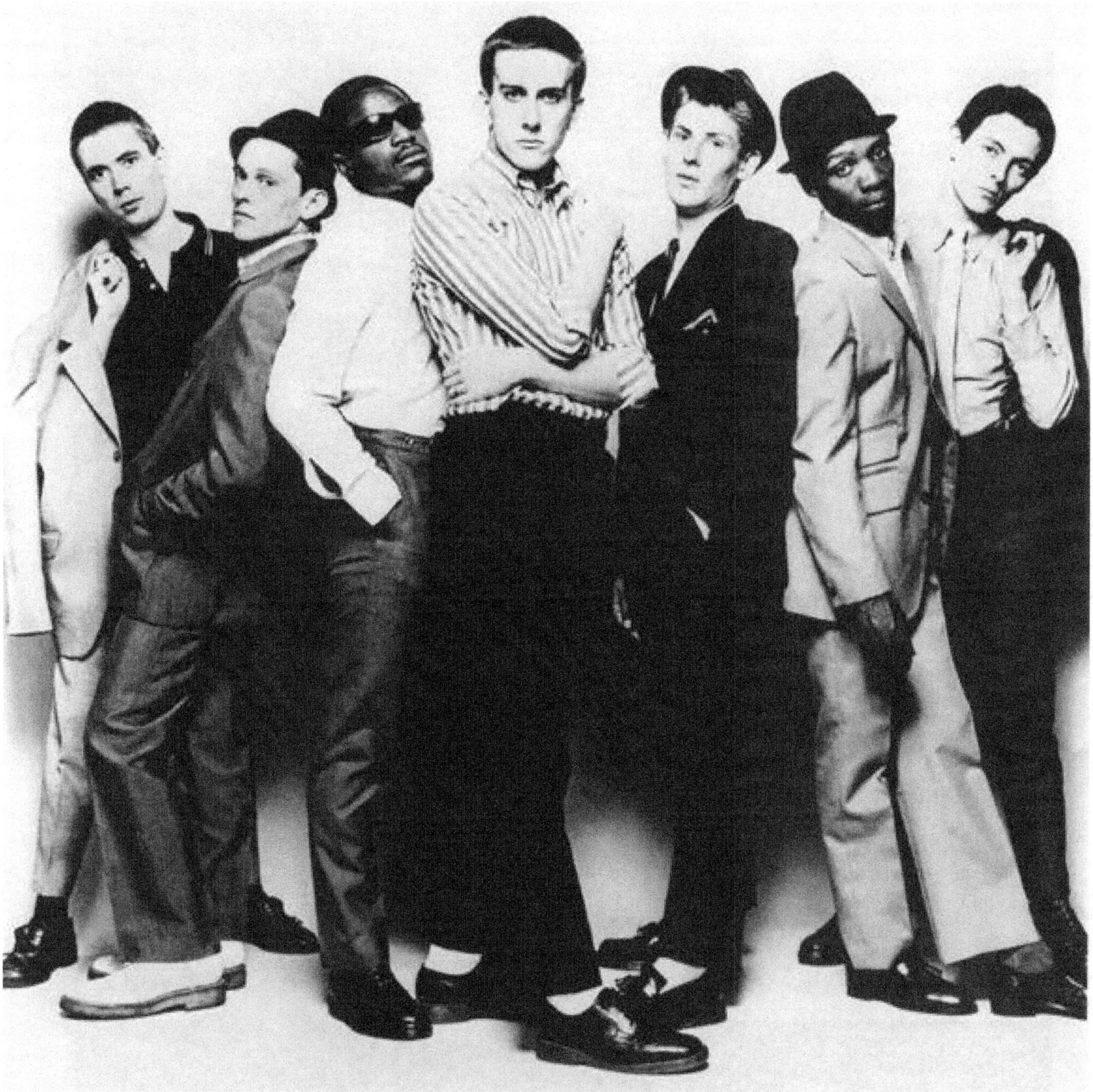

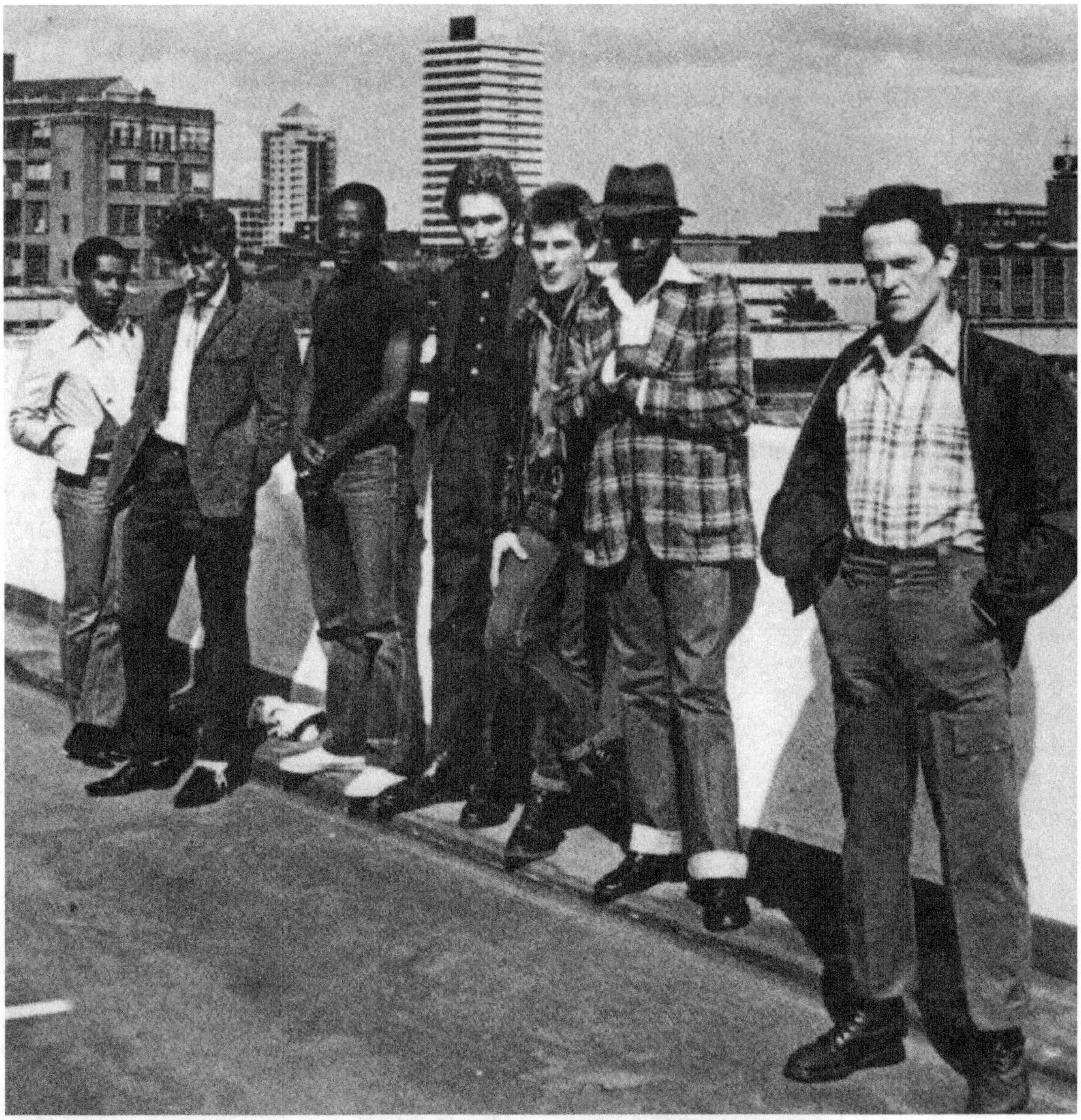

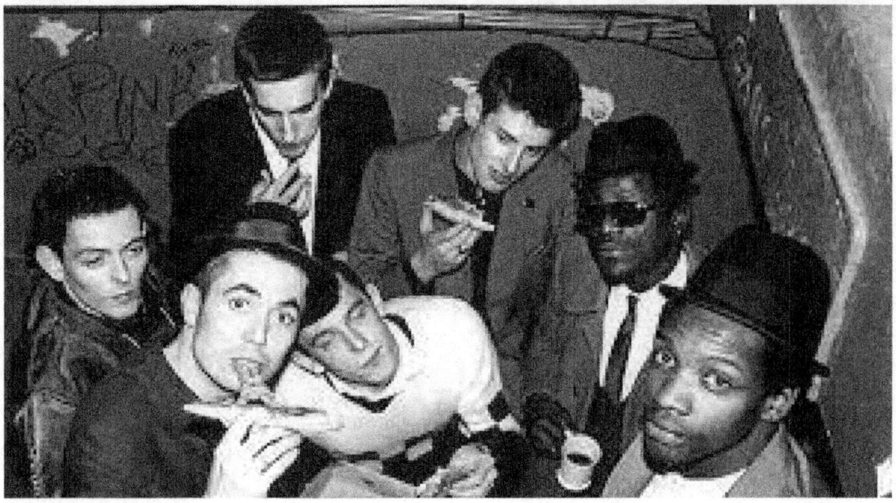

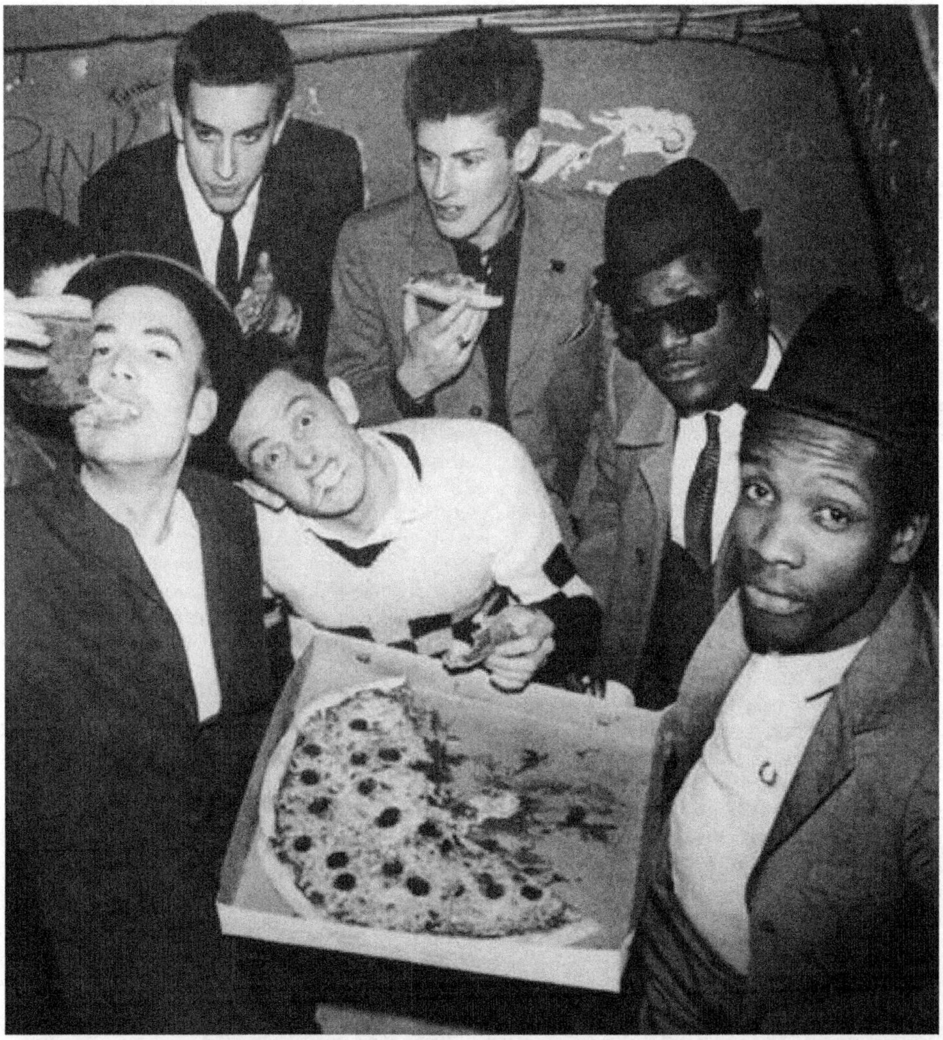

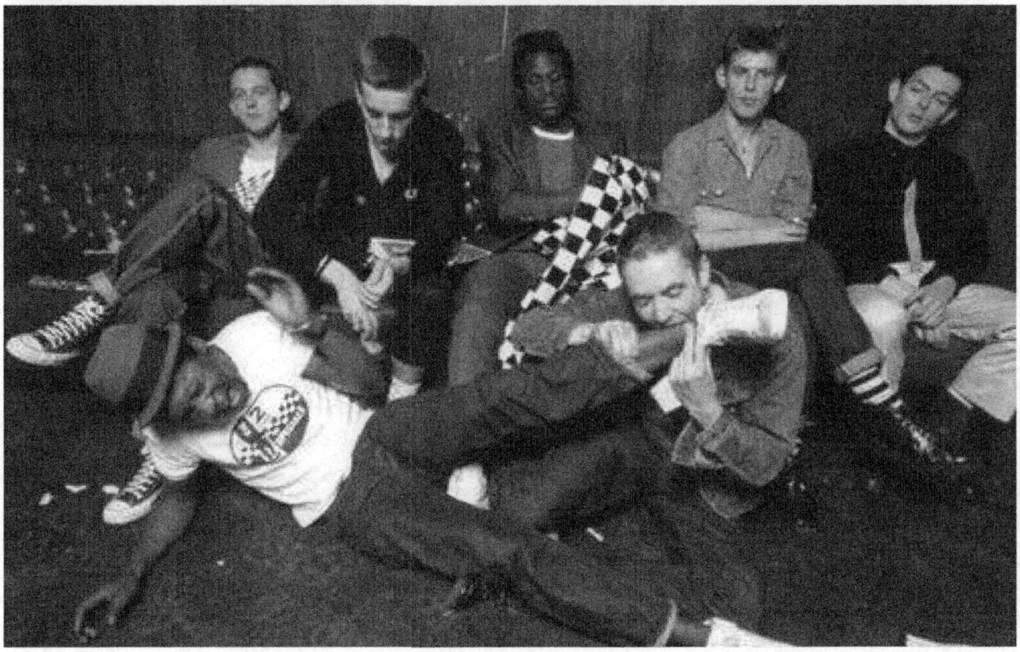

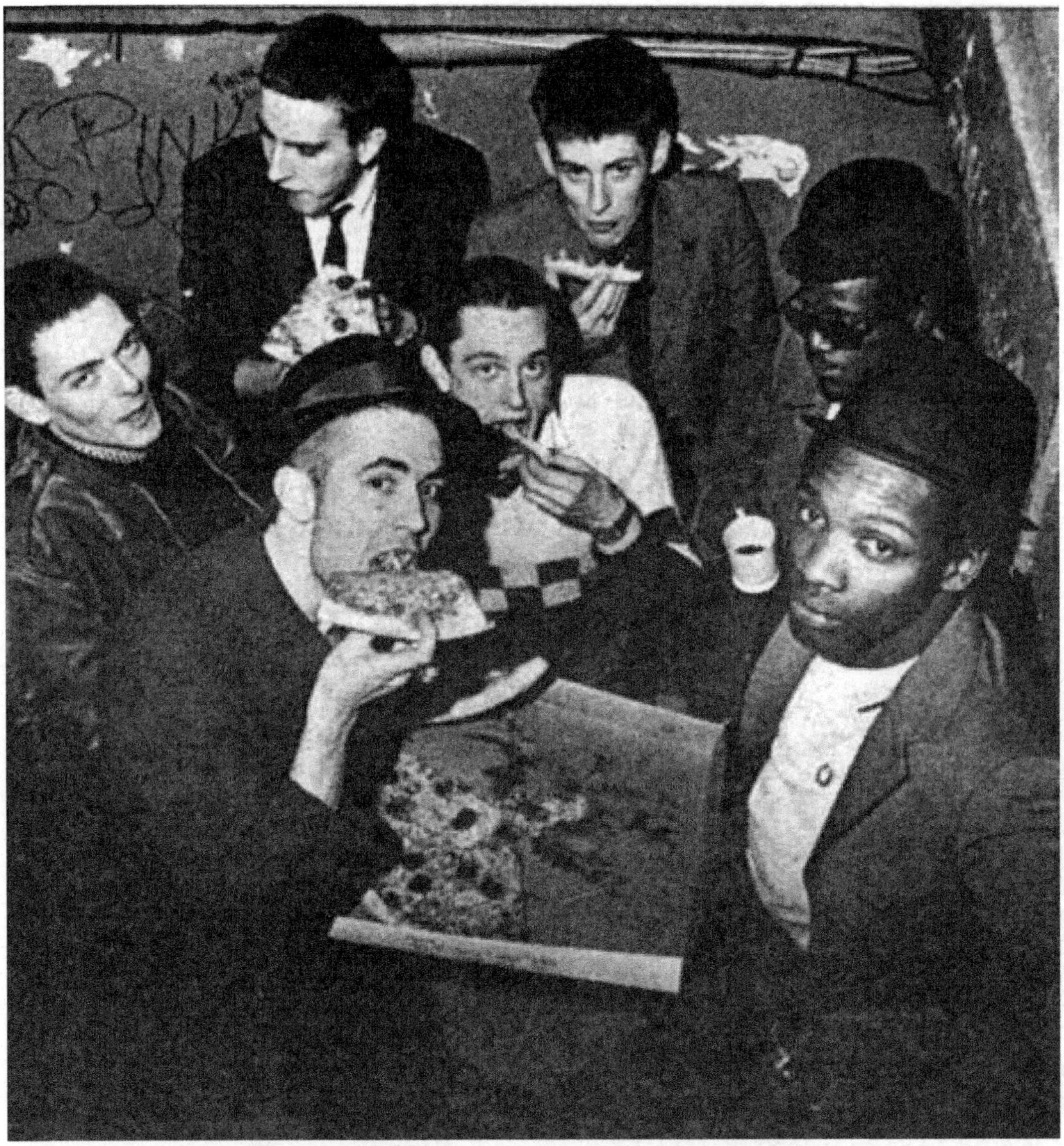

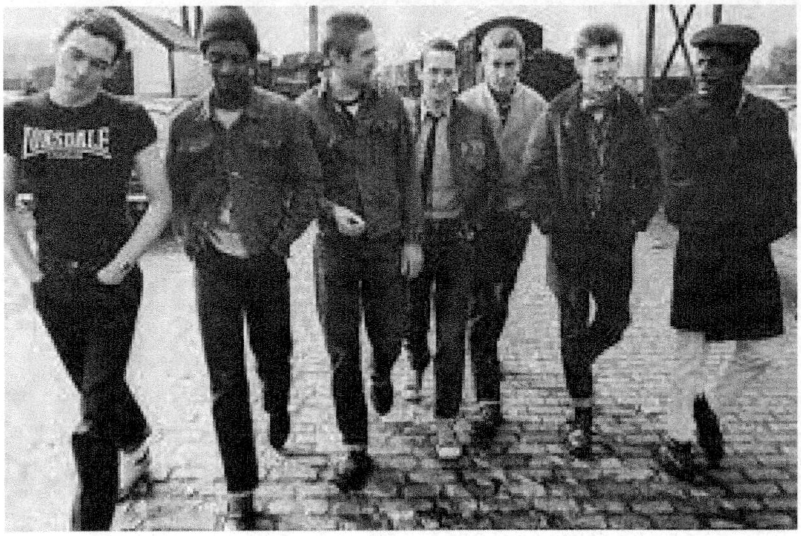
LONSDALE

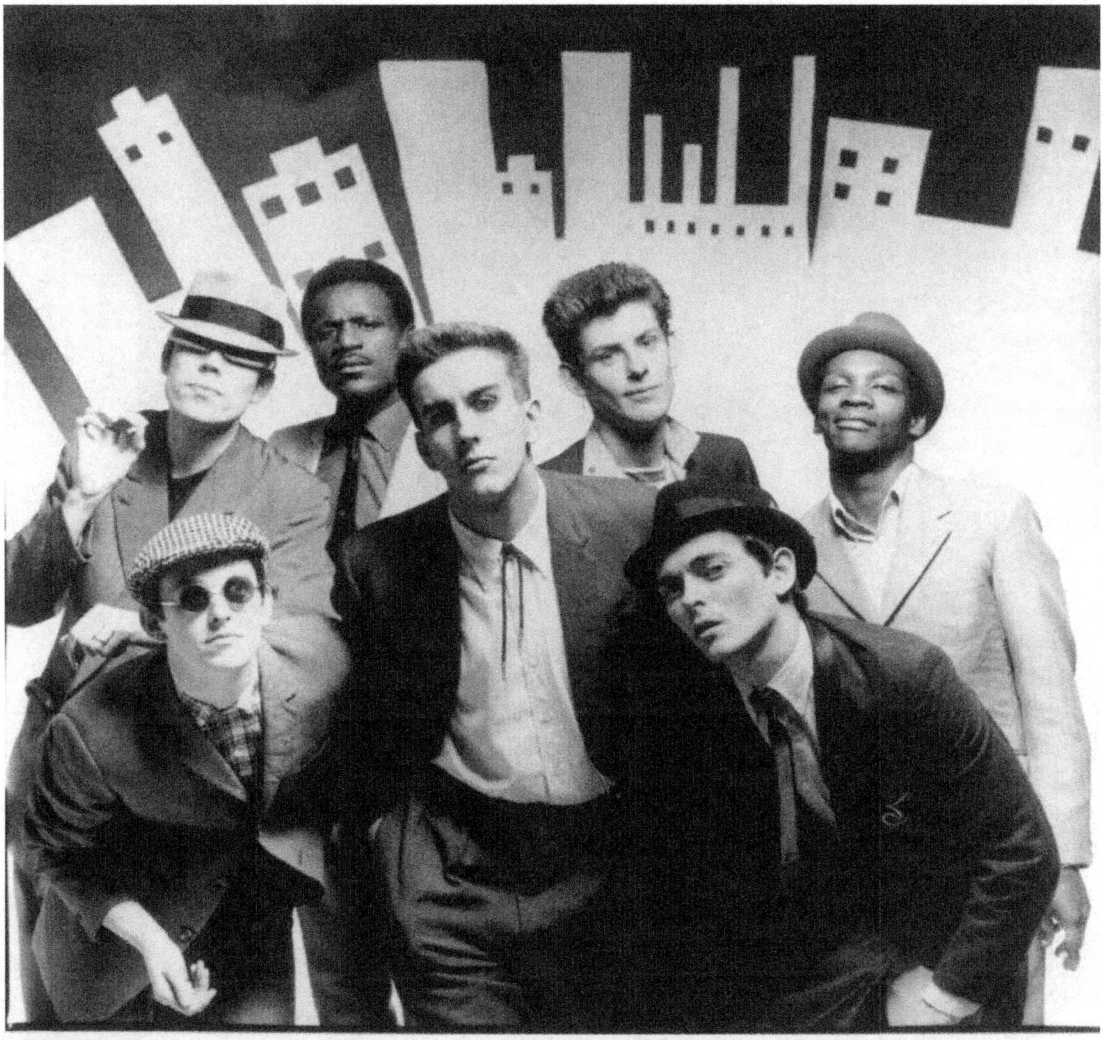

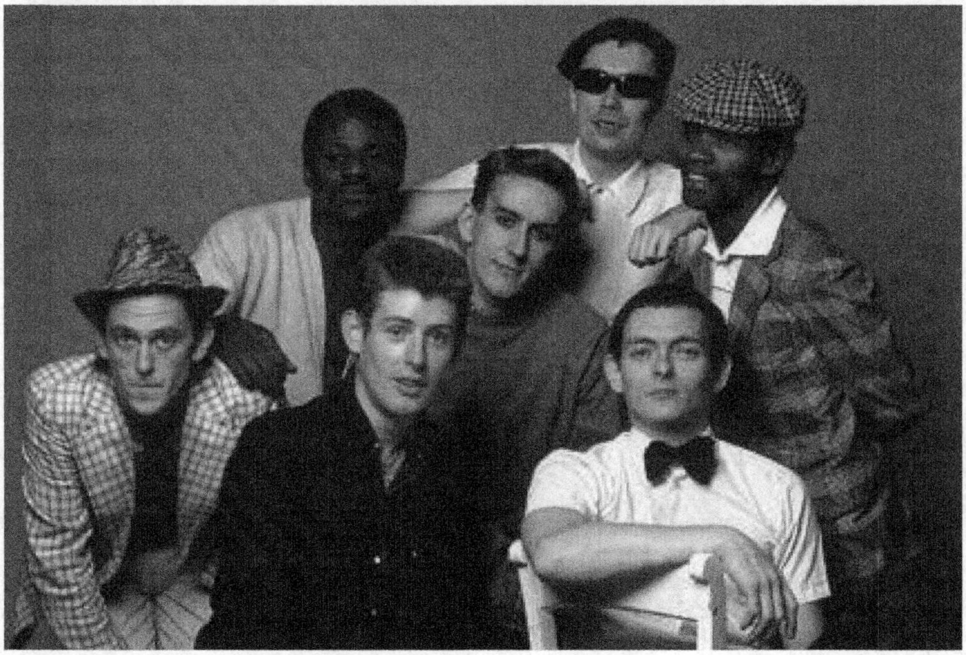

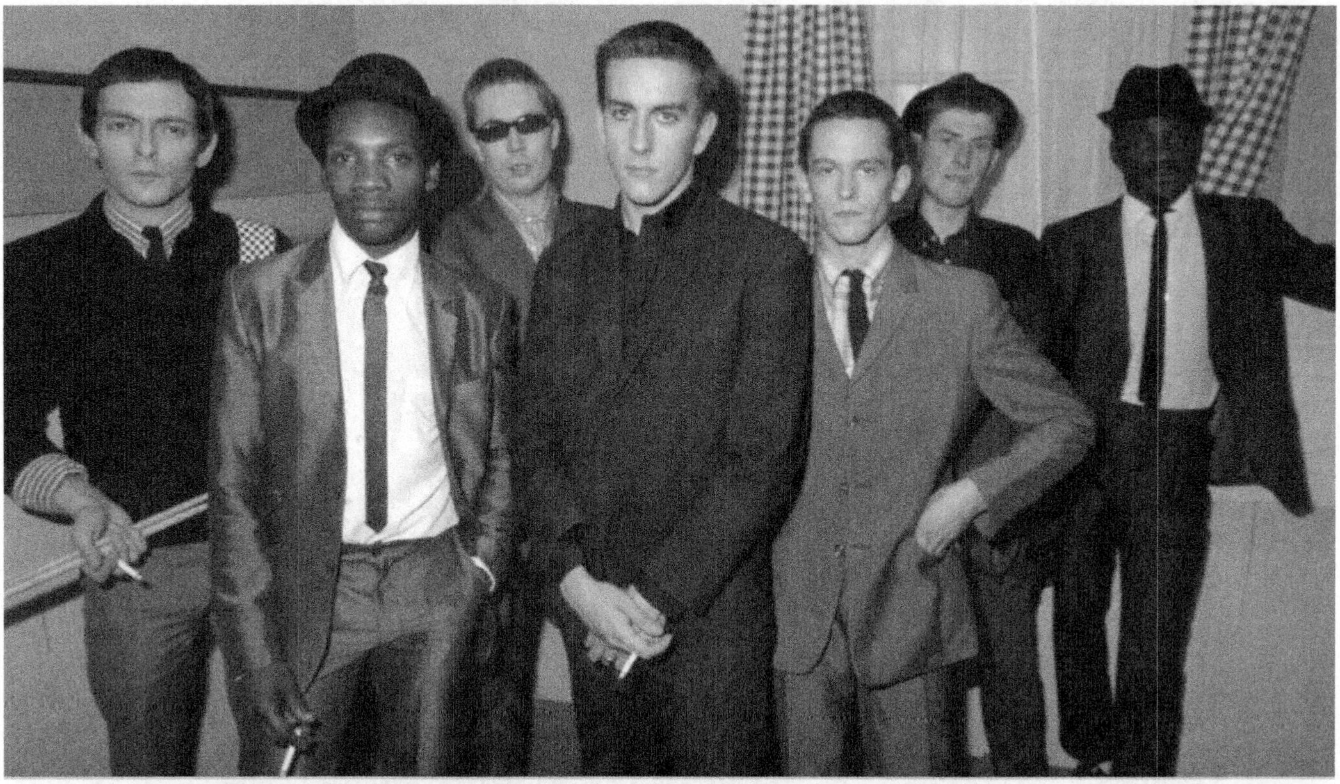

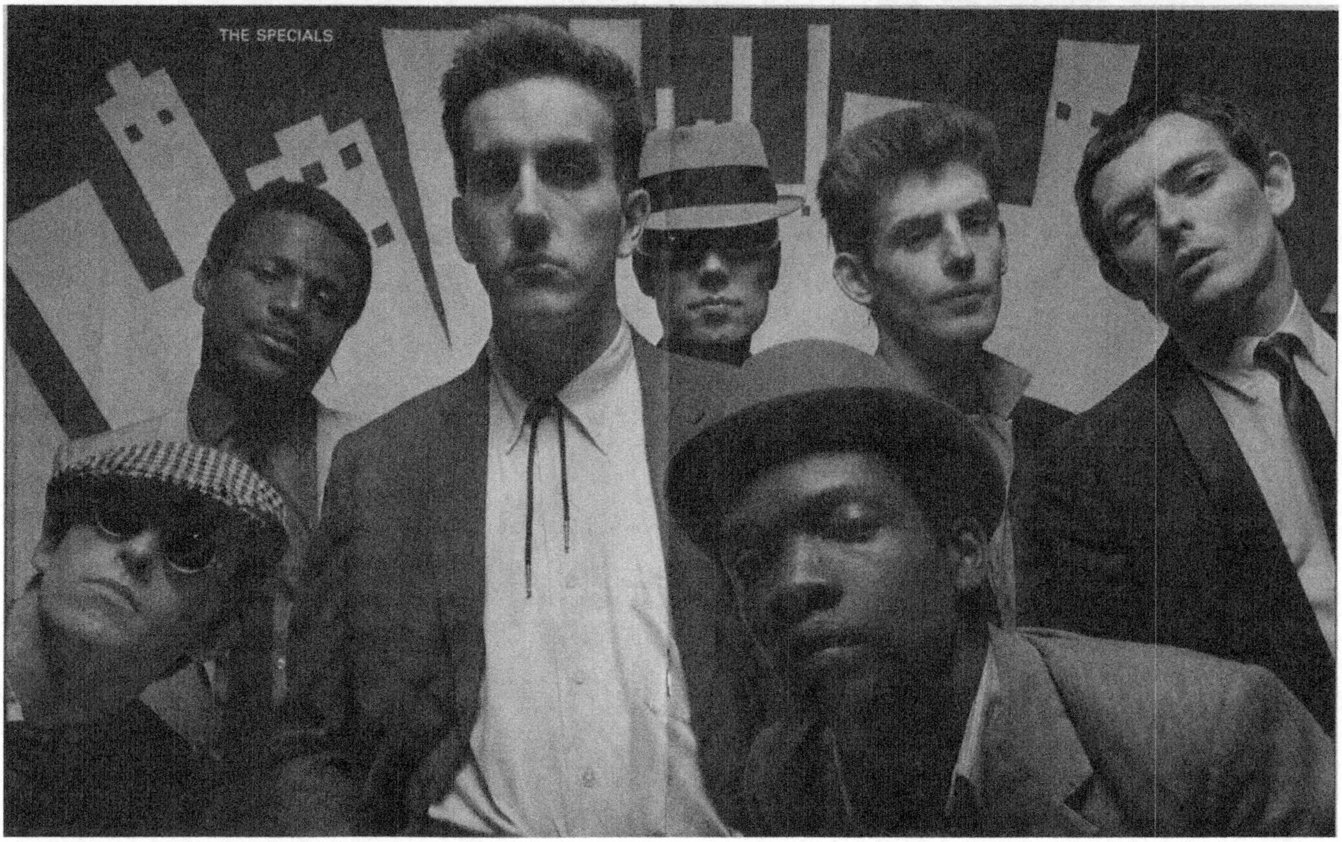
THE SPECIALS

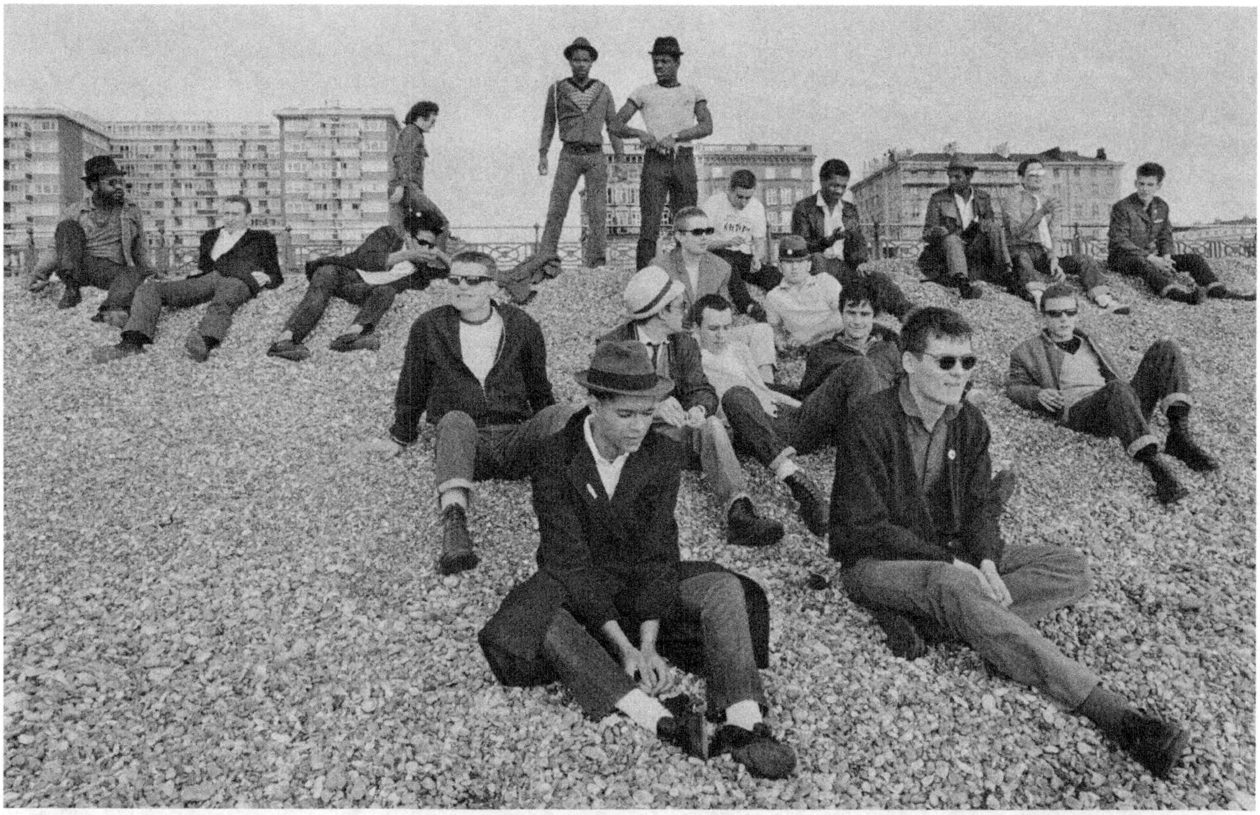

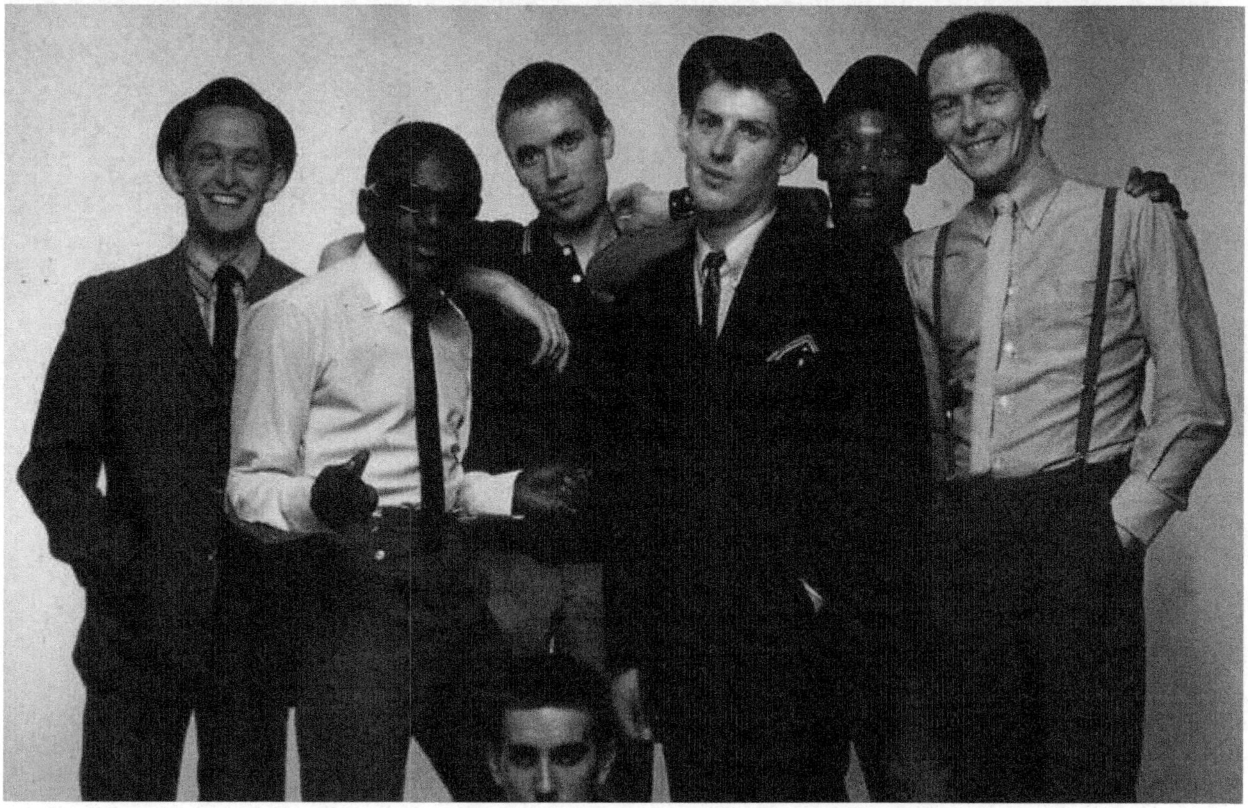

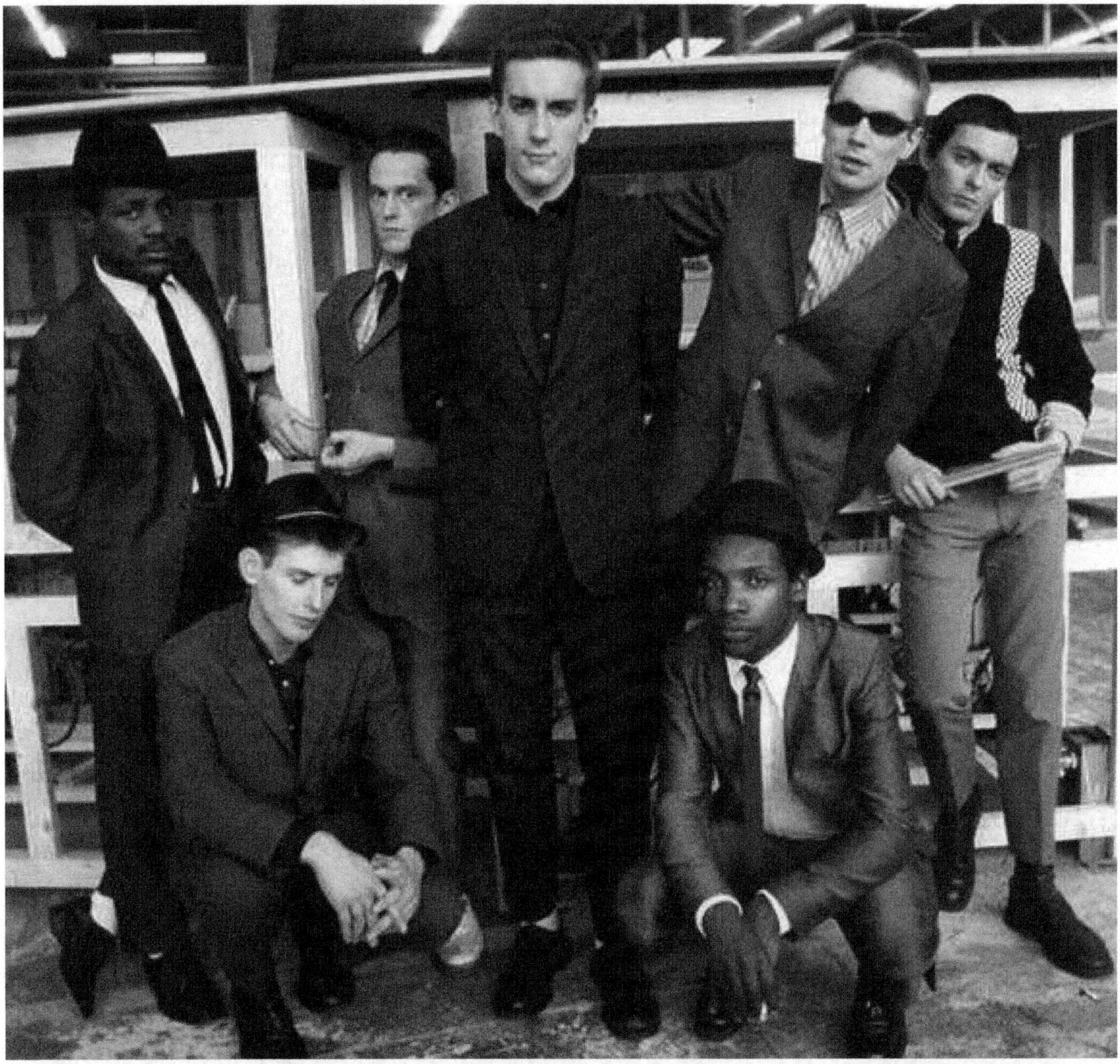

THE SPECIALS

76

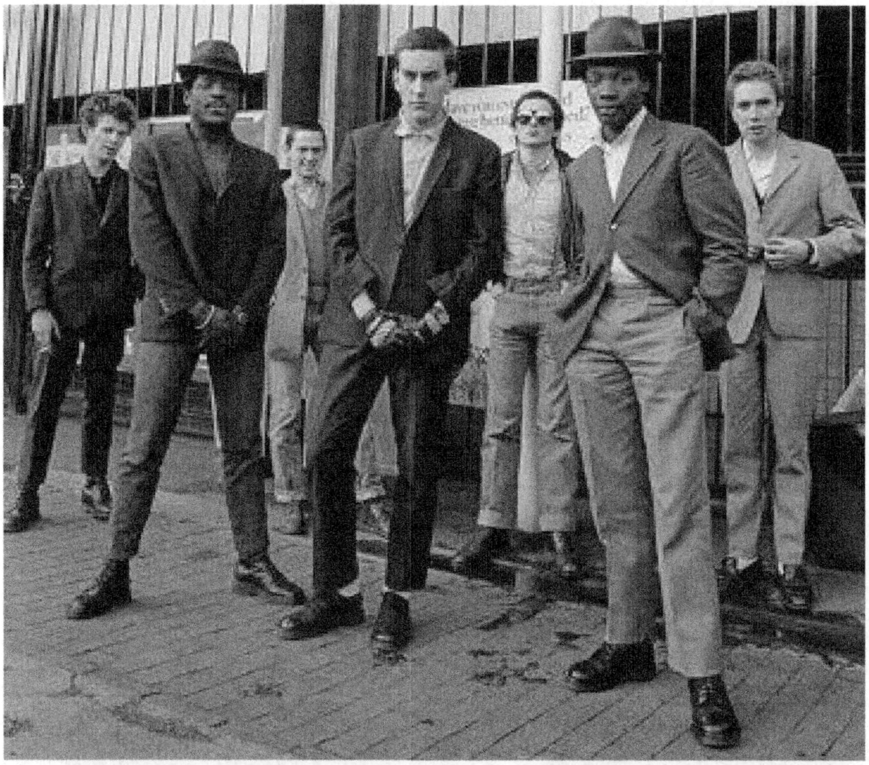

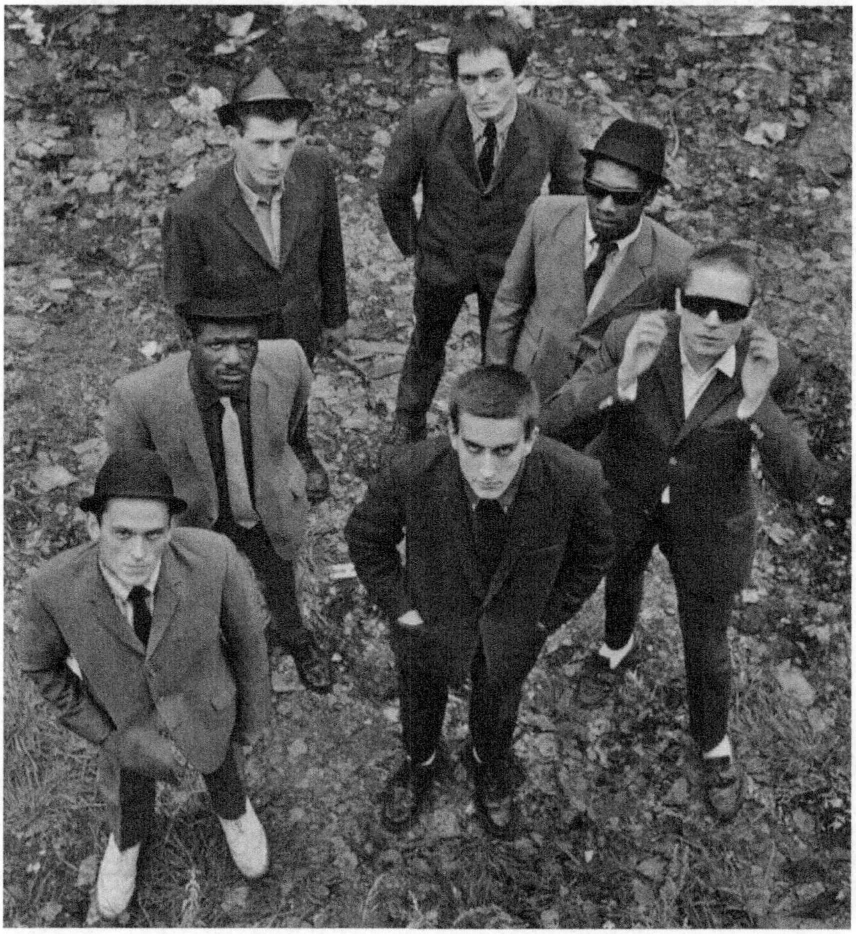

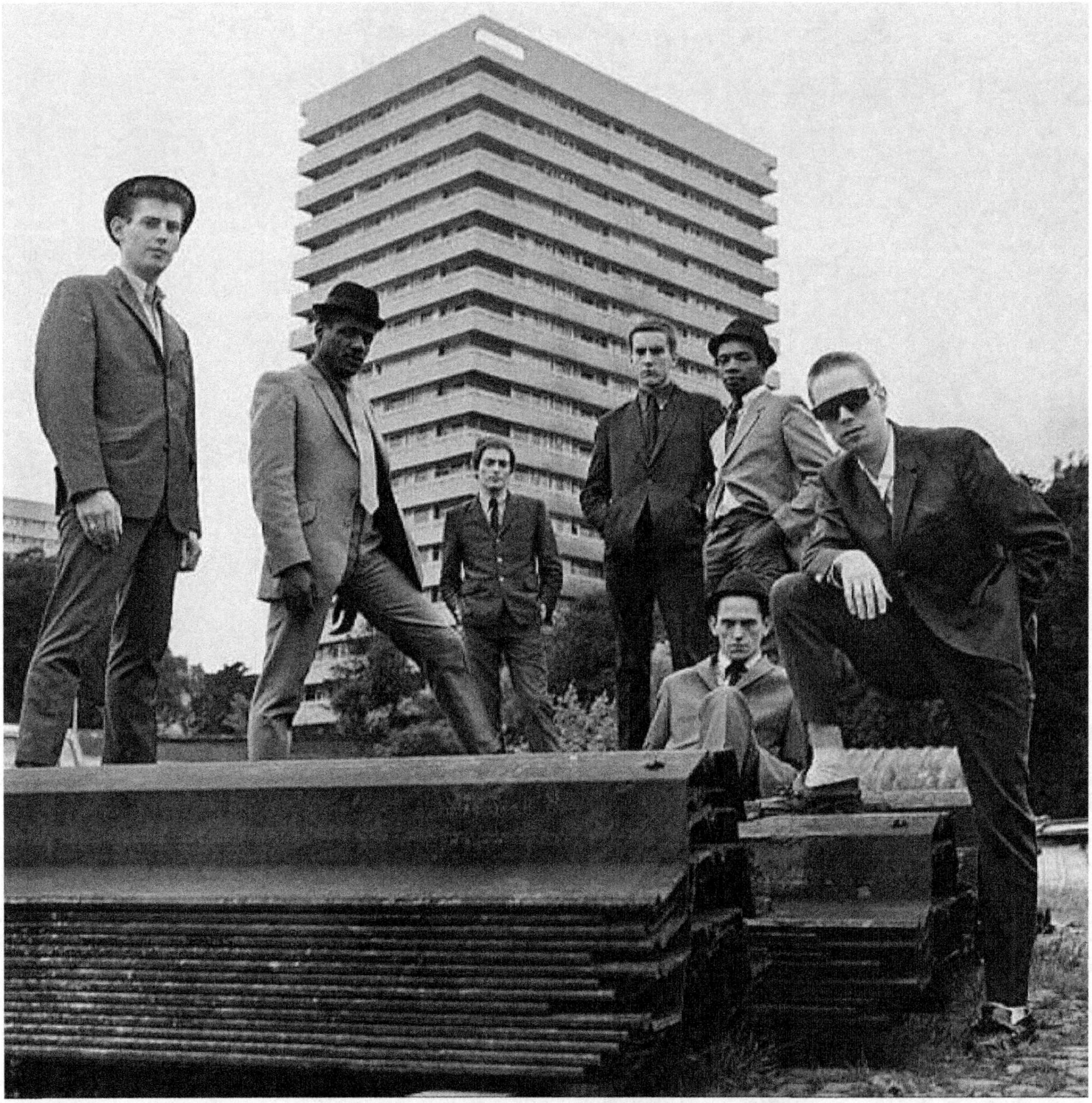

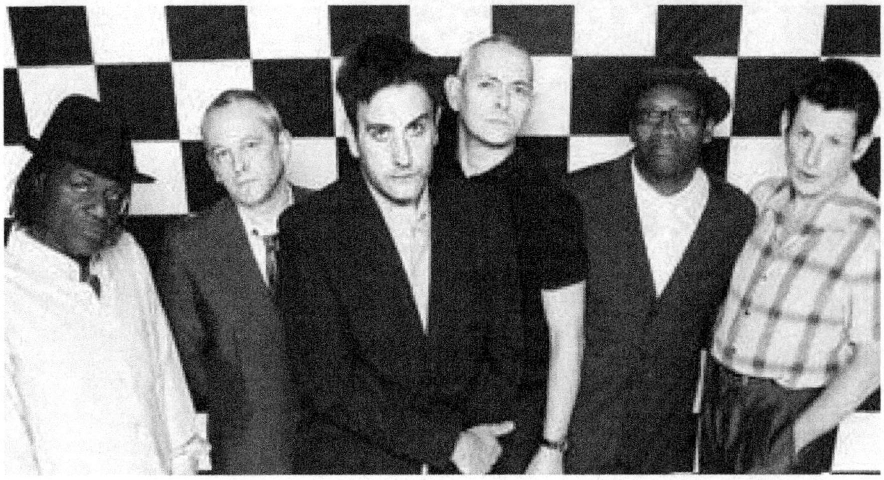

79

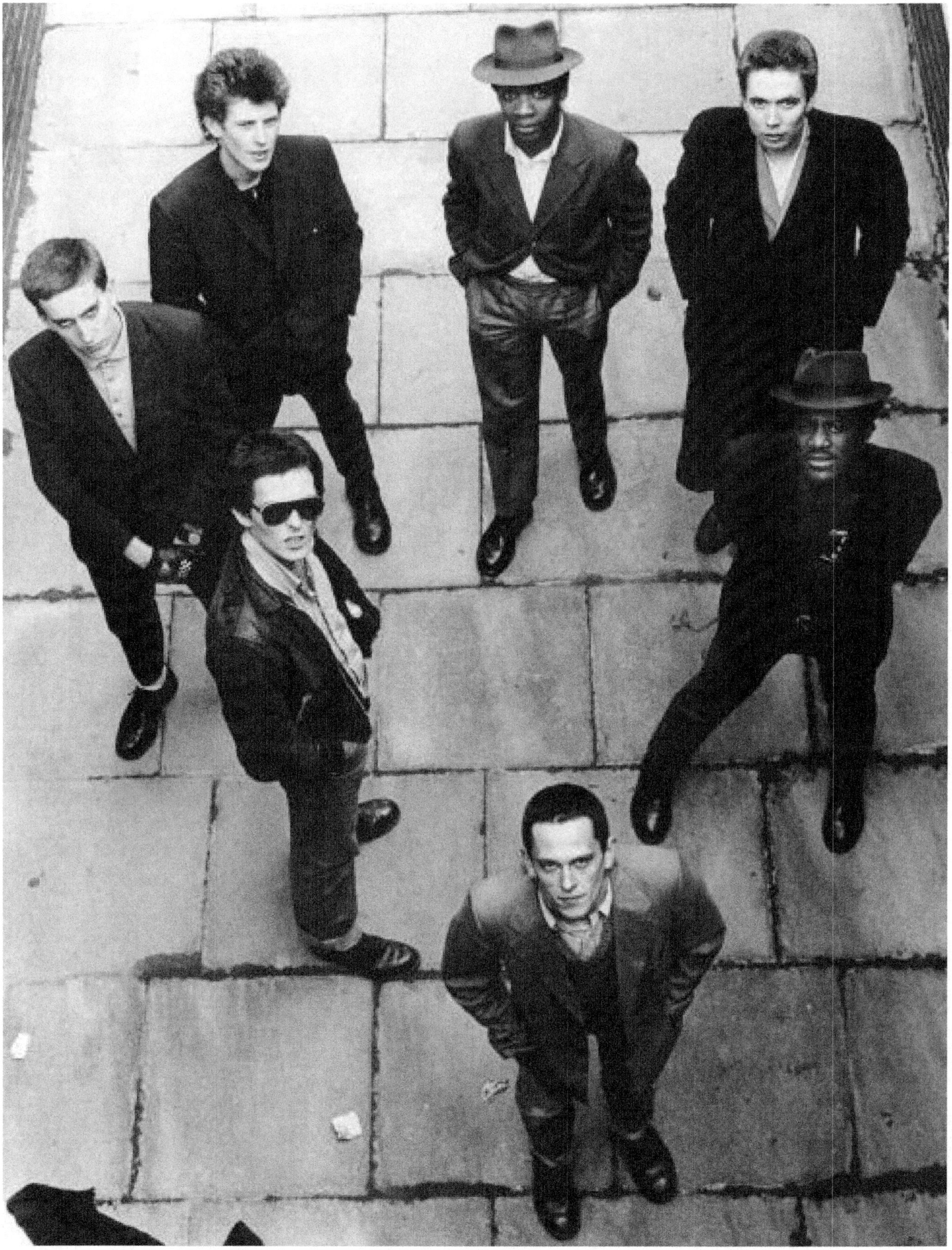

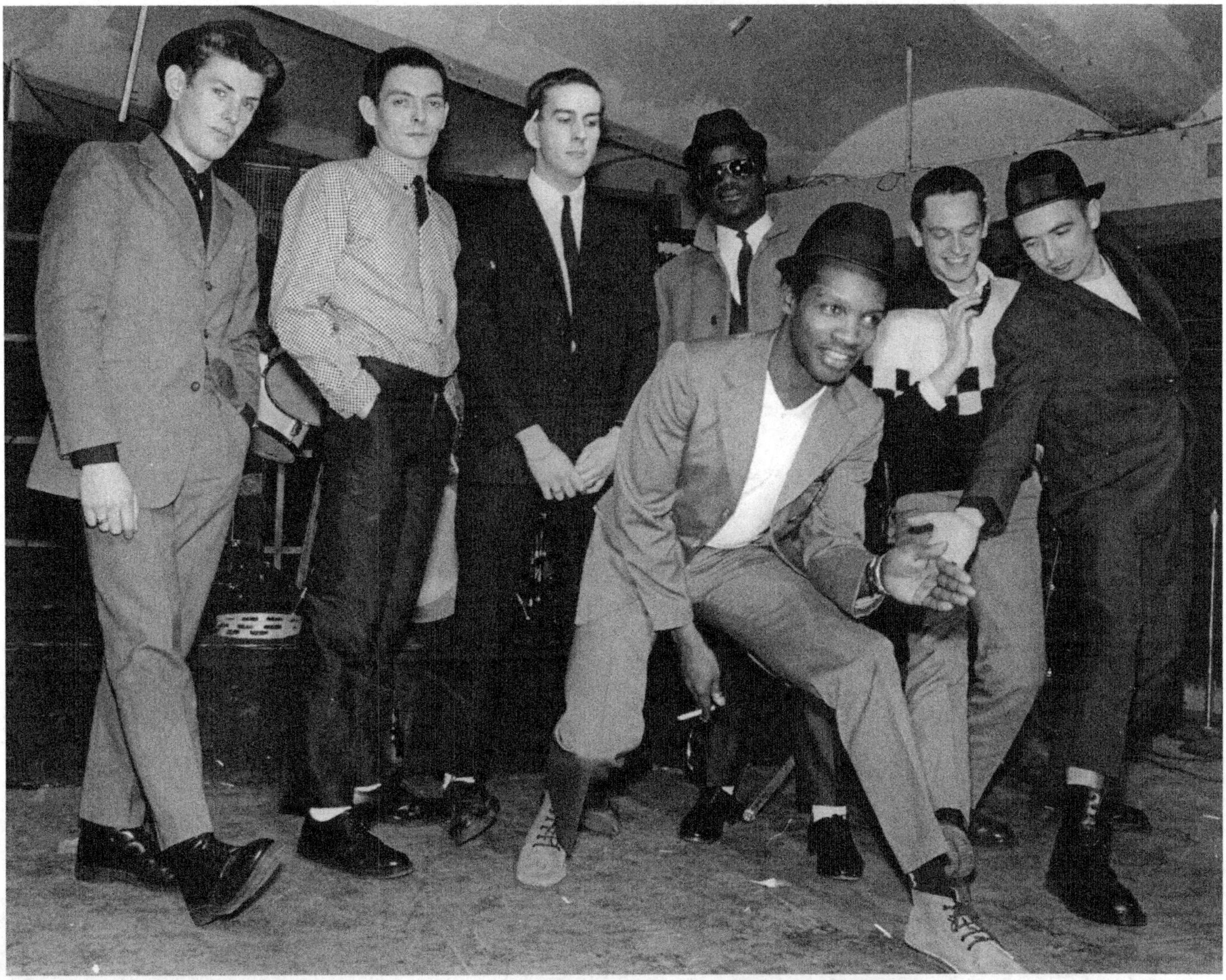

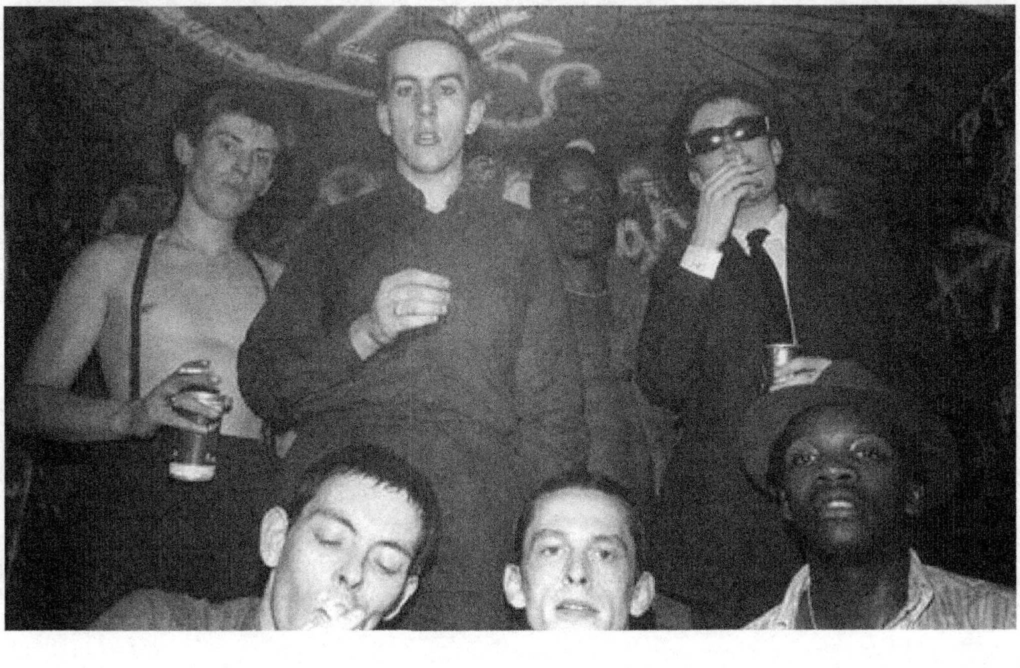

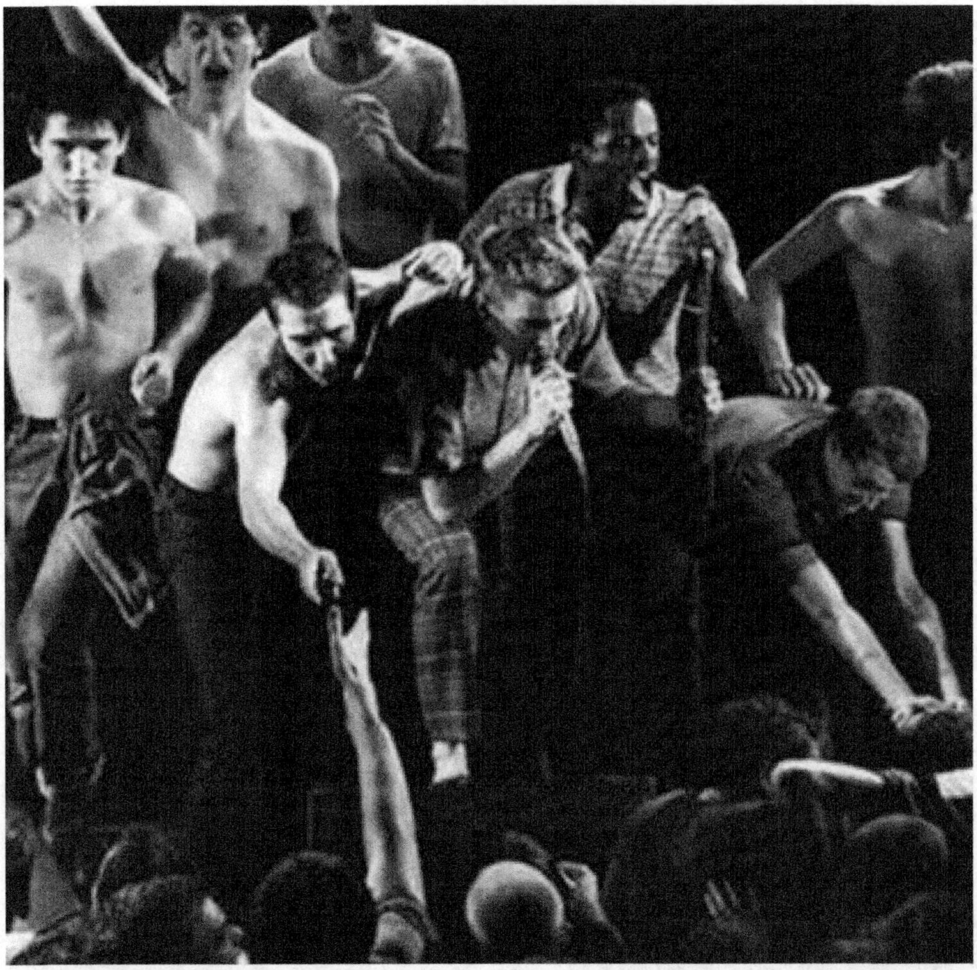

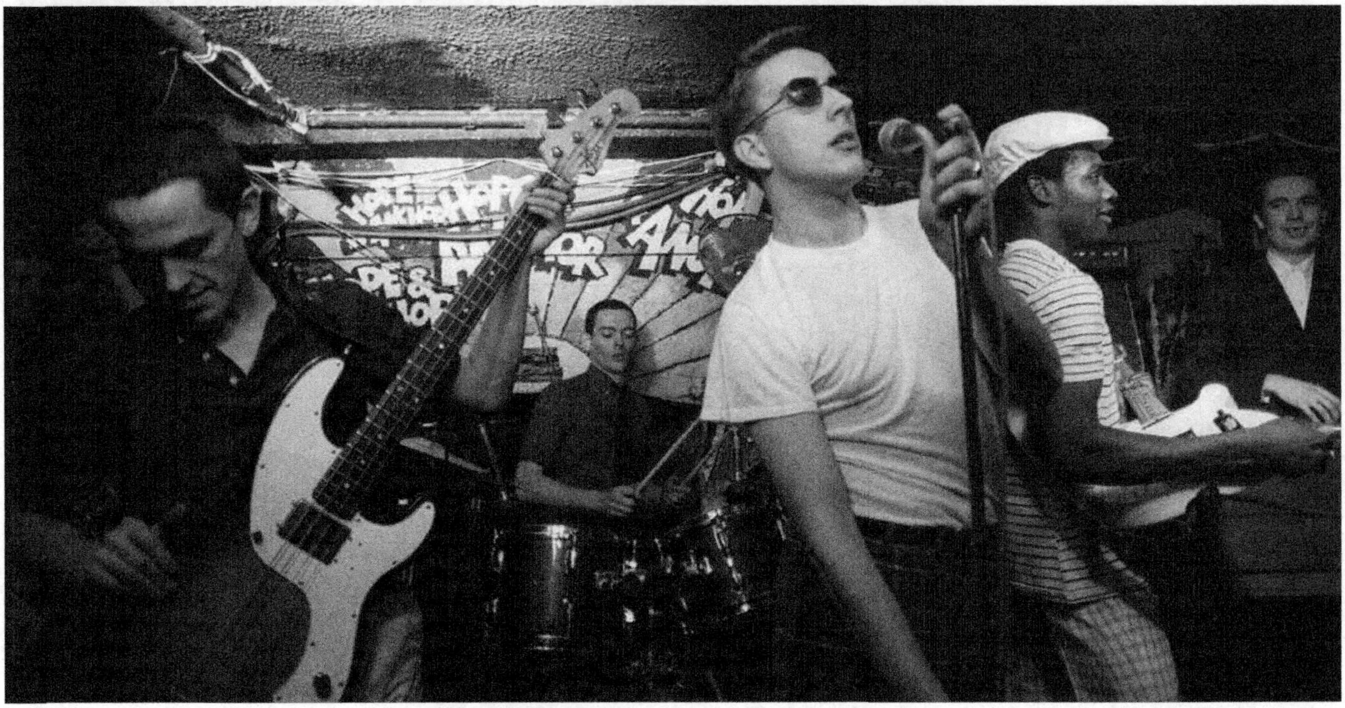

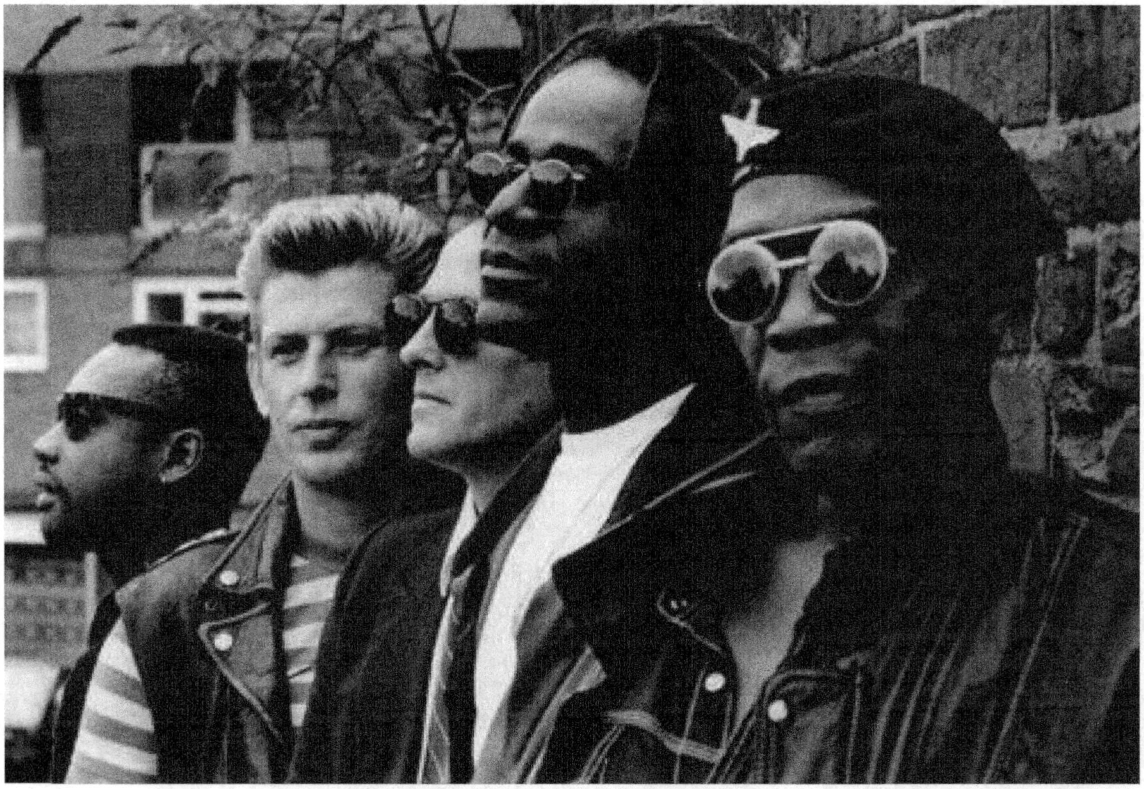

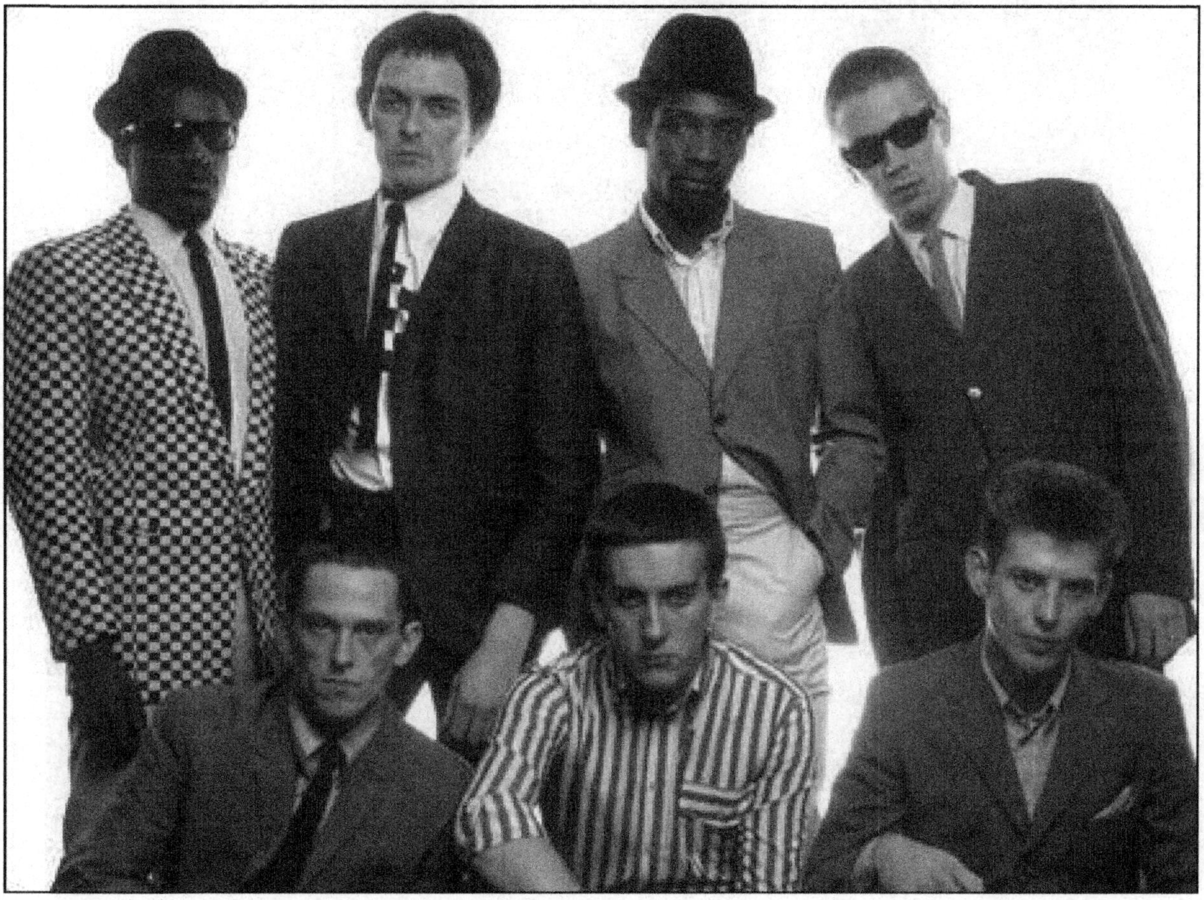

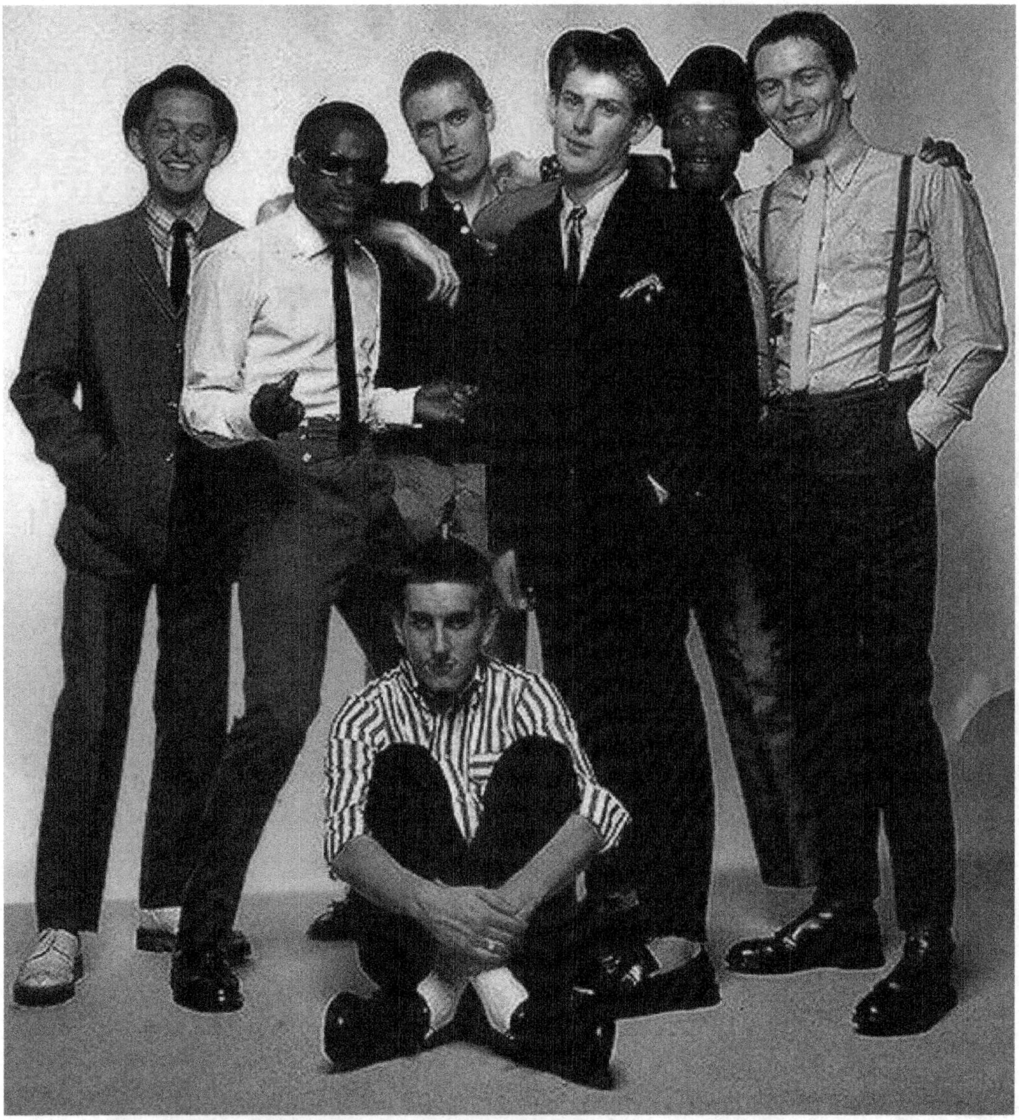

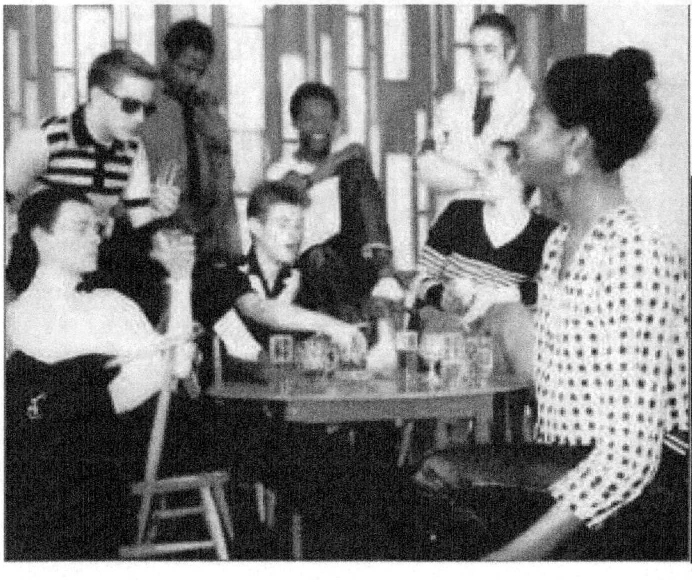

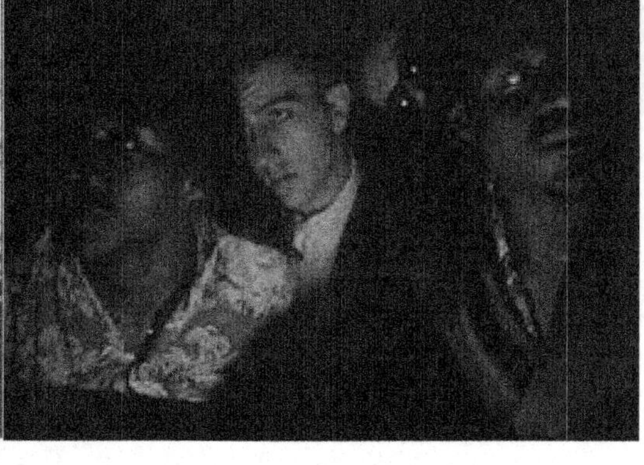

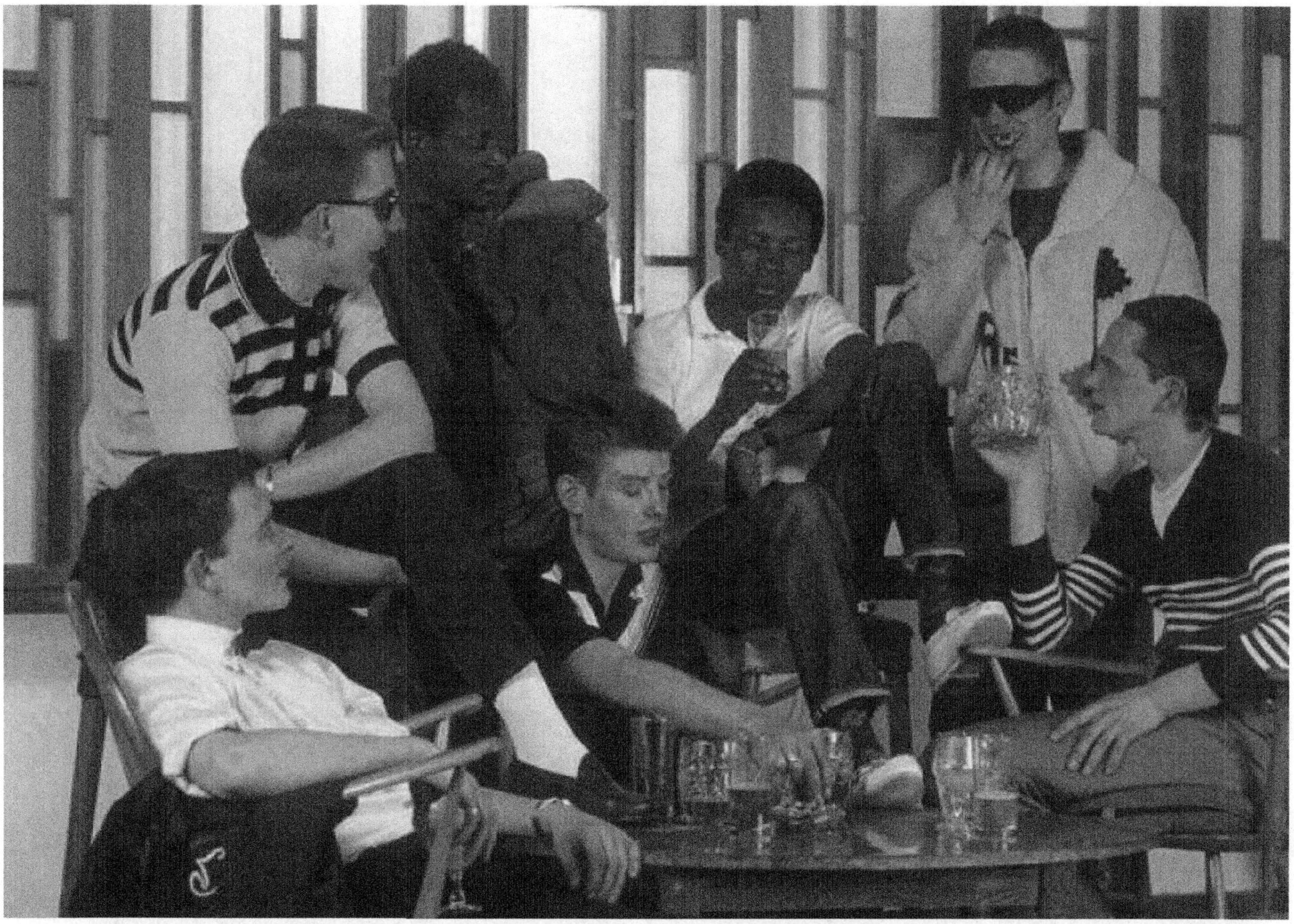

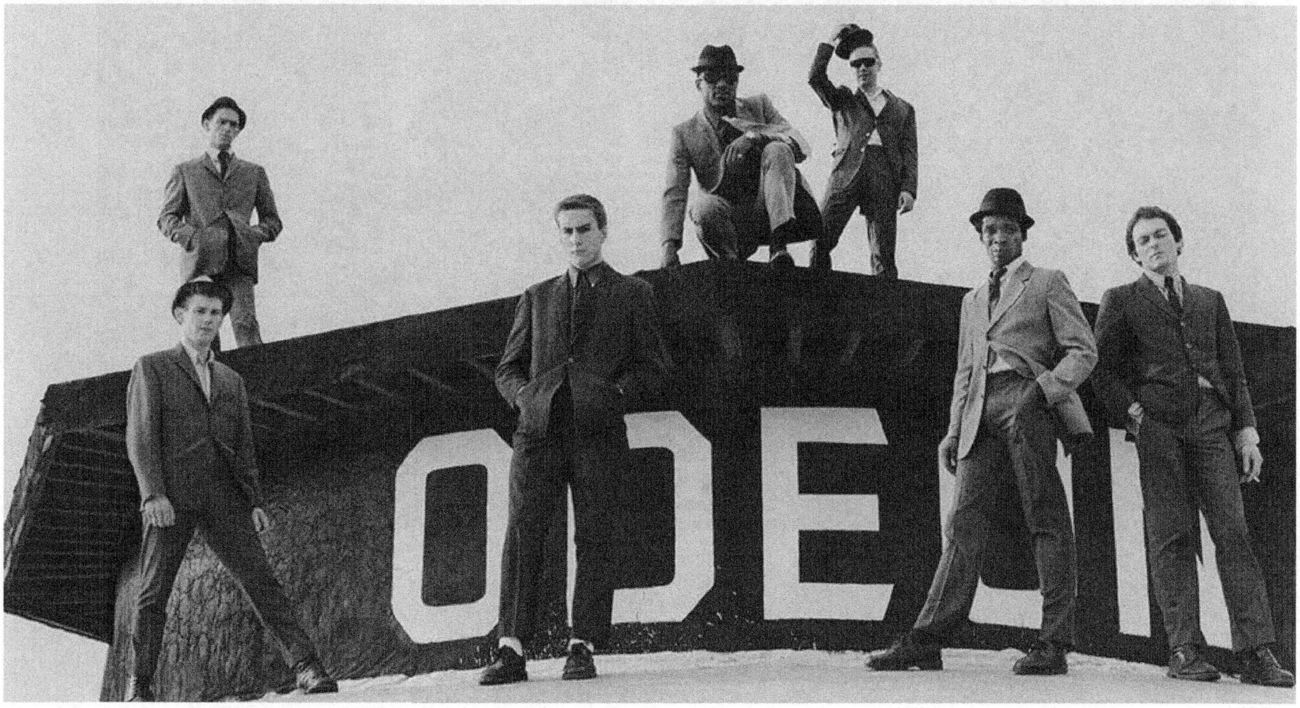

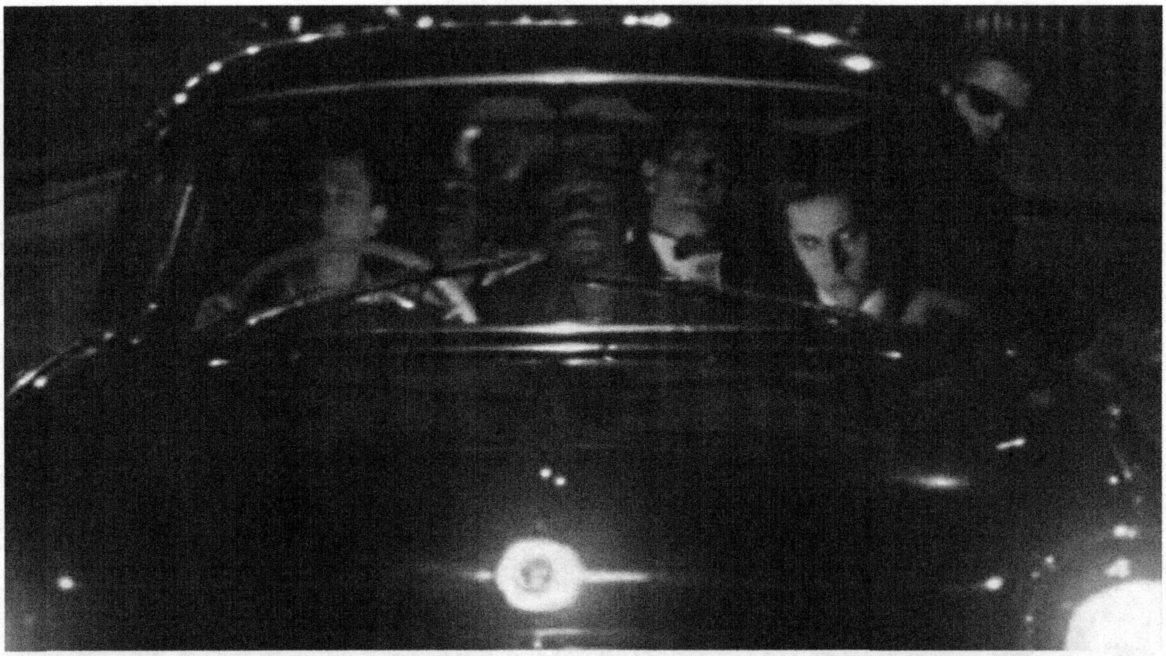

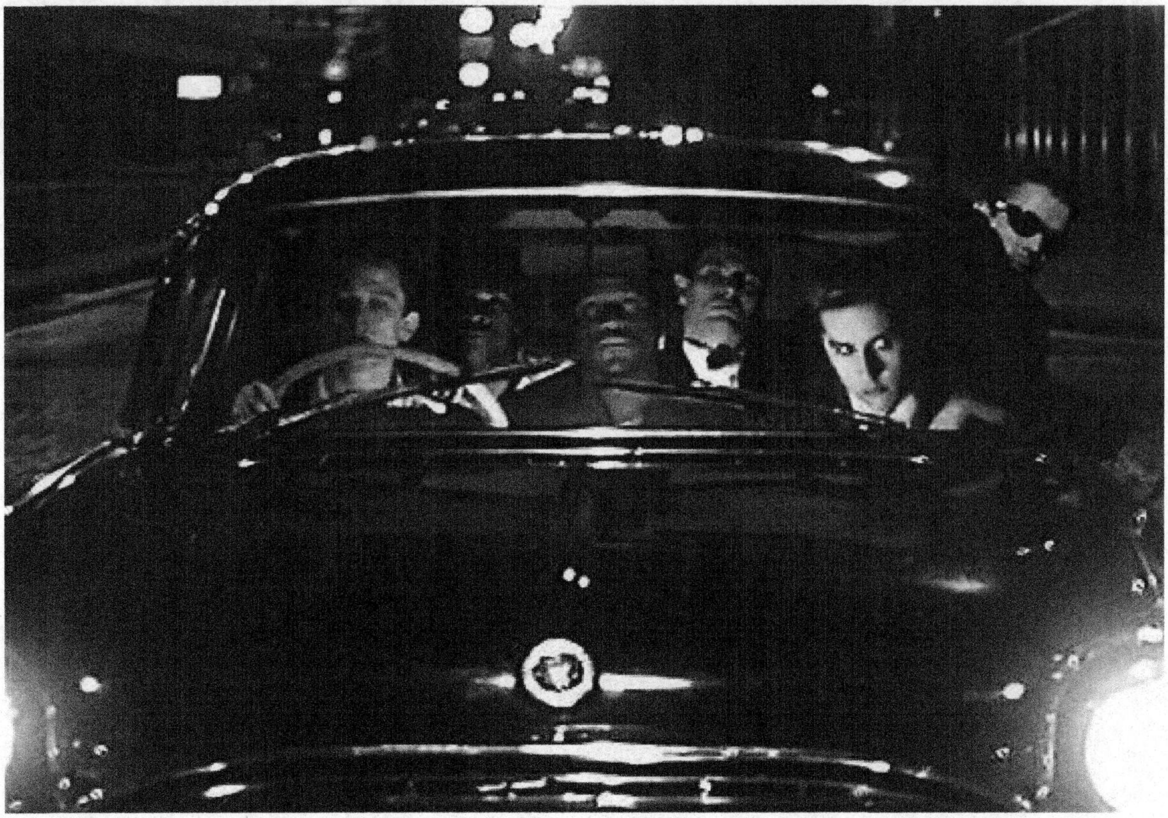

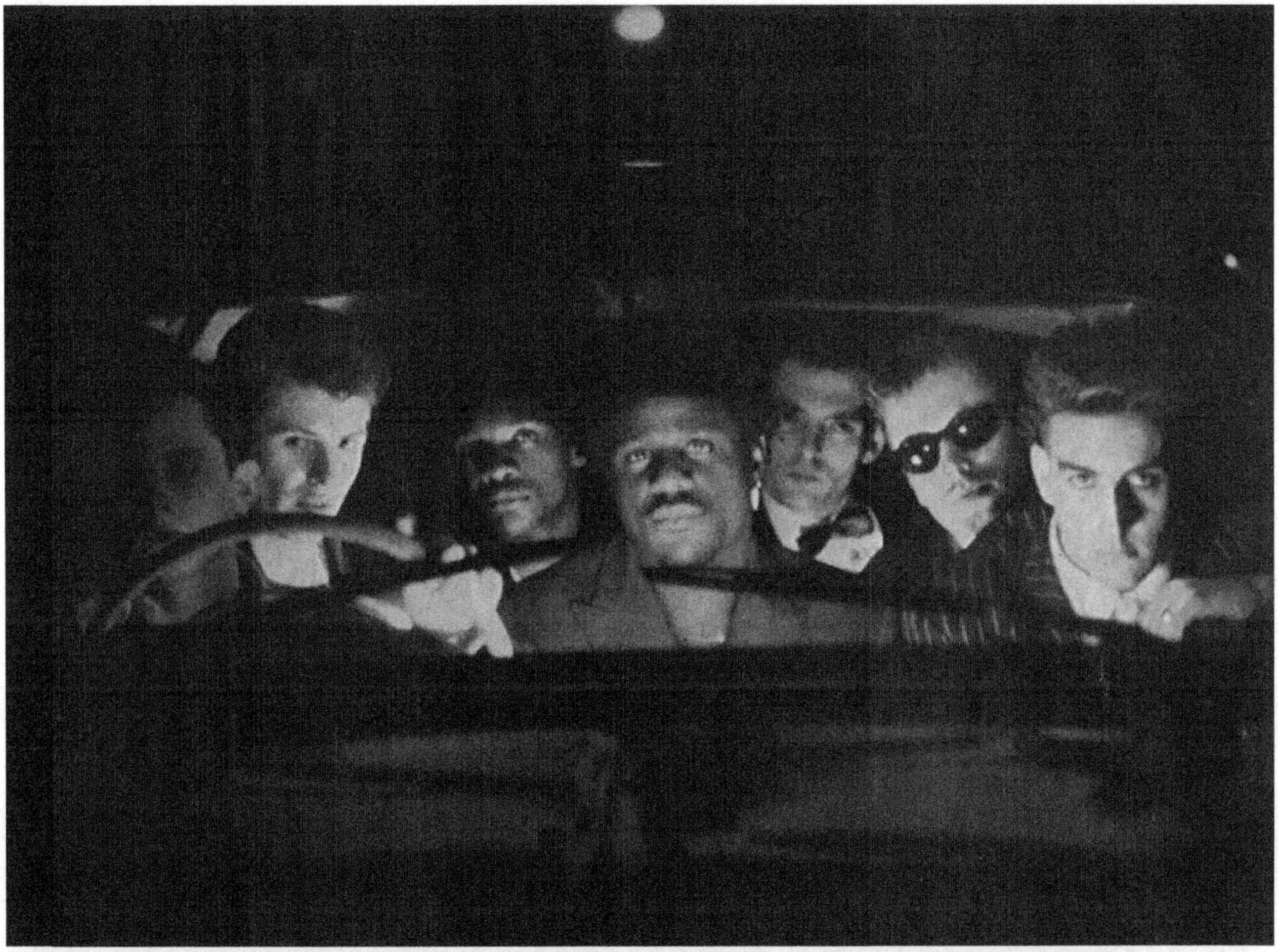

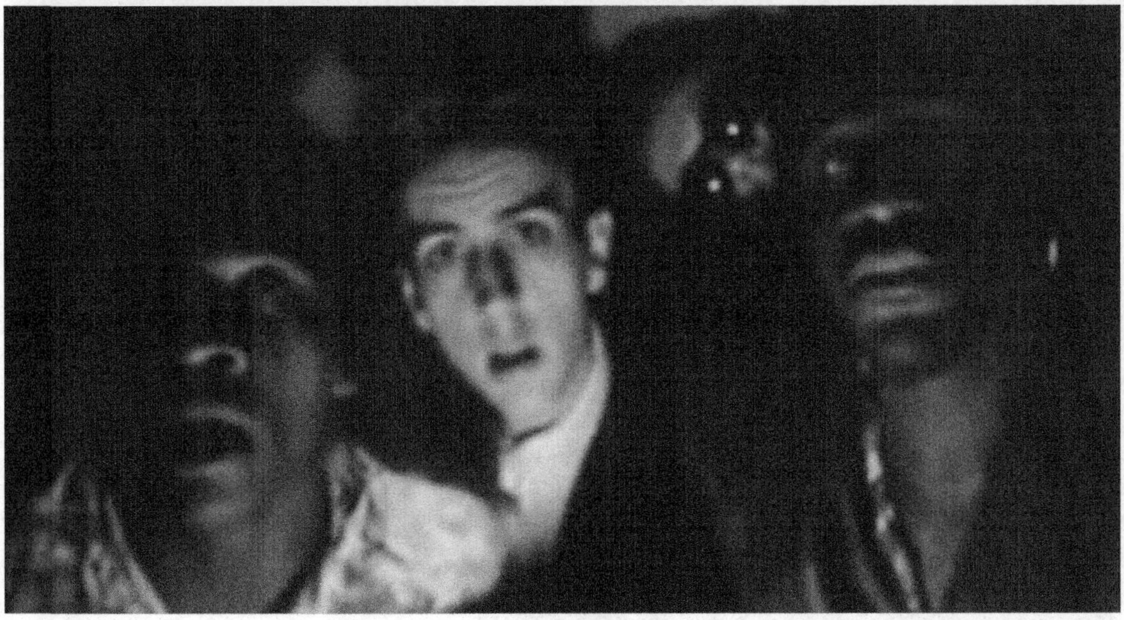

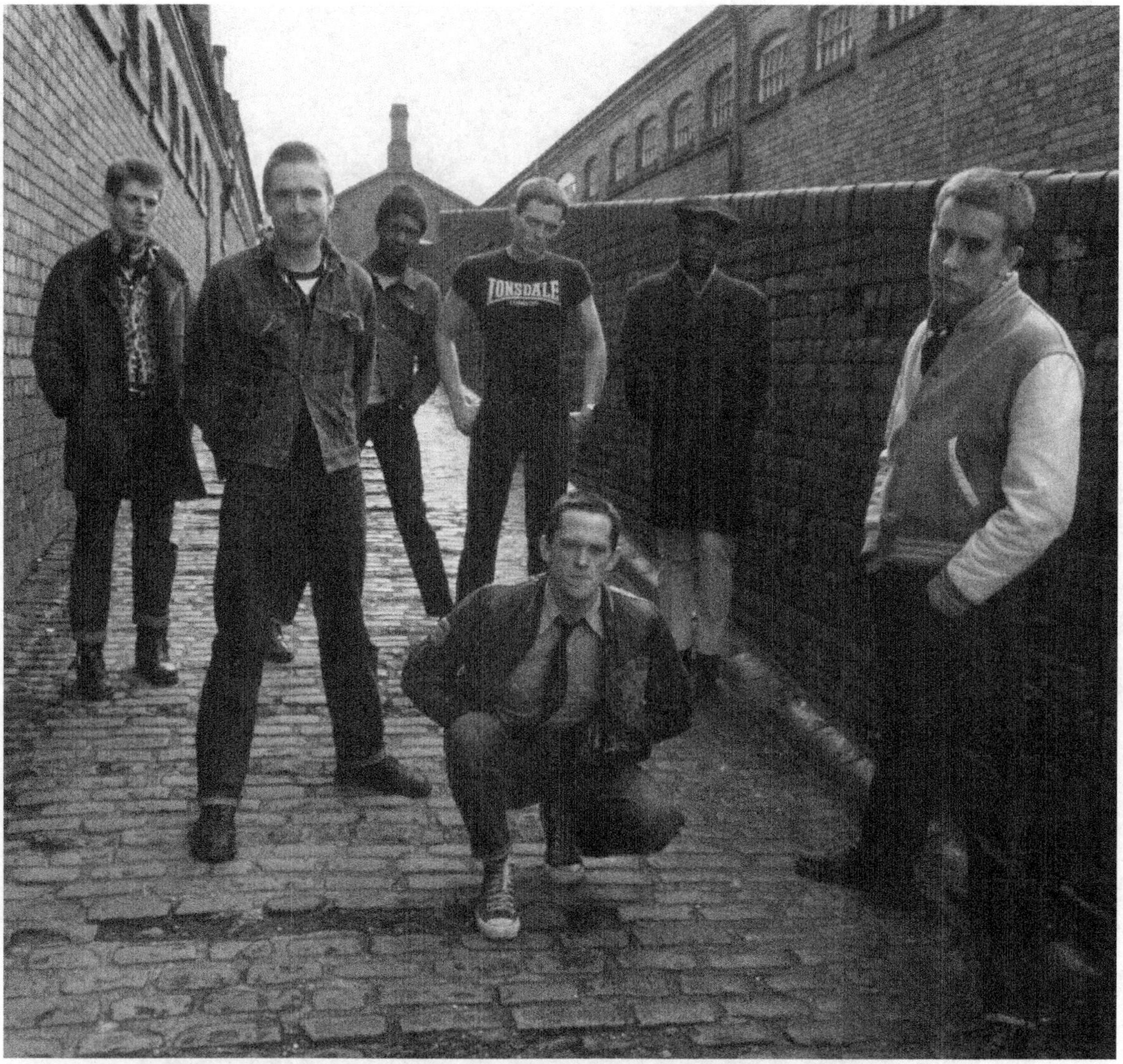
LONSDALE

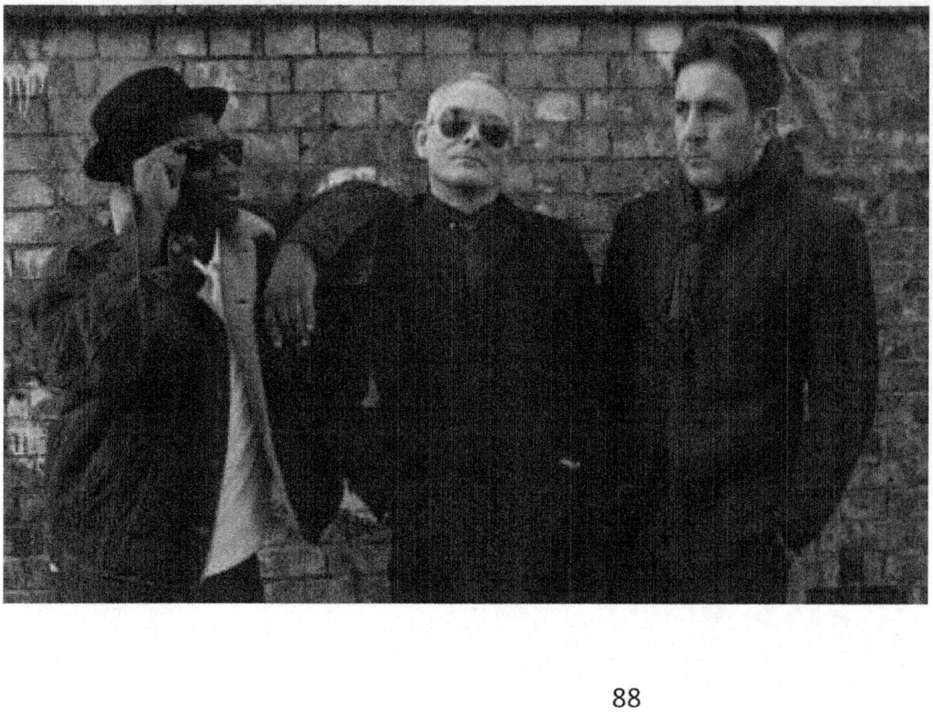